BAY TO OCEAN

2019

The Year's Best Writing from the
Eastern Shore Writers Association

D1115489

EASTON, MARYLAND

Cover photo: "Verrazano Bridge to Assateague Island at Sunset" by Bob Balestri. This image is licensed in perpetuity by the copyright owner, Bob Balestri, to the Eastern Shore Writers Association at no cost for the sole purpose and use as the cover of the Bay to Ocean 2019 anthology and the normal usage in promoting this publication.

Contents

PREFACE

One of the many reasons I love the mid-Atlantic region is the diversity found in its compact boundaries: Major cities, ski resorts, crops and herds, salt lapped beaches, and surging rivers feeding two economically and ecologically important estuaries. From my hometown, Baltimore, a three-hour drive or less delivers you to completely other worlds: the peaks and hollers of Appalachia, the sometimes-not-always genteel South, the sometimes-not-always stoic North, and the bogs and inlets of the watery Shore.

I've heard the nickname "America in Miniature" applied to this region due to this topographical and cultural variety. Over the course of my career, I've made the case that it is also "America in *Literature*." Writers like Roger Alan Skipper leaning into his Appalachian roots and Martha Grimes mining her childhood memories at a western Maryland lake resort; David Simon, Rafael Alvarez, Anne Tyler, and John Waters exploring the gritty, ethnic, middle class, and unreal sides of Baltimore; John Barth, Priscilla Cummings, Helen Chappell, Lucille Clifton, and Tom Horton turning salt air into children's books, novels, poetry, and nonfiction.

Yes, all of America is explored by its literary artists, but there's just something about the shore ... and the writers gathered here know it.

My paternal grandmother lived on the northern edge of Kent Island, and as a boy I recall the precarious cliff that the Chesapeake constantly chewed not far from her house. As a boy himself, my father—who split his coming-of-age years between city and shore—took the old Smokey Joe Ferry from Light Street to Love Point, where a popular hotel welcomed summertime guests and year-round drummers (salesmen). For me, and for all of us who write about it or from it, the land between the bay shore and the ocean is unique. Its Algonquin peoples remembered, its oyster beds tonged, its fields harvested, its channels plied, its beaches combed. Blue crabs and blue hens. First State and Free State, which means a lot of history. Emphasis on the word *story*: ones this place gives us and ones we bring to it.

The writers collected in this anthology contribute to the quality and diversity worthy of the region's nickname. These brackish writers—a mixture of natives and newcomers, as is the mixture of river water and seawater in estuaries—remind us how the human condition follows us no matter our station in life, regardless of the landscape. In poetry and prose, these are vignettes of family lost and time lapsed, abuse suffered and trauma survived, nature engaged and worlds eroded, endless childhood summers that too quickly become too short as we grow older. These writers navigate this shifting terrain and ruminate on life before washing up on its beaches.

We are reminded that even in paradise, life is not always idyllic. It ebbs. It flows. But there's always something to be learned, something to be shared. Reading the pieces in this anthology is like knifing a shovel into a wet ocean beach and overturning a sand-dollar, page after page.

Welcome to the Eastern Shore of "America in Literature."

Gregg Wilhelm
Summer 2019

FICTION

James Burd Brewster

THE OLDEST BROTHER

"Are we really meeting our oldest brother?" asked five-year-old Timmy. He looked up at his older brother and then darted ahead of the group.

"Yes. Finally," said Peter, a high school junior. "Hey, don't get too far away."

Timmy banked left, flew a tight corner, and lined up in formation next to his brother. Peter immediately reached out, grabbed Timmy's hand and held on tight as Timmy pulled against him, making their arms straight. Whenever he did this, Peter always felt they looked like a tanker refueling a plane in mid-air and their arms were the fuel boom connecting the two planes.

"What will he be like?" Hope's question was quiet and soft. Peter put his un-tethered arm around his younger sister's shoulder and gave her a reassuring hug. New situations made his twelve-year-old sister under-confident and as a result, shy.

"He will be just like I told you. He's our brother and loves us very much, so he should be a lot like us. Isn't that right, Mr. John?" Peter glanced to the man leading them down the corridor for confirmation and then looked behind them to make sure they were not being followed.

"Let me carry you, Timmy," Mr. John replied. He stopped, stooped down, and scooped Timmy up, settling him on his hip like a pro. "What do you think an oldest brother should be like?" he asked Timmy.

"He'll be just like Peter said. He'll be big and tall and will wrestle with me and give me piggy back rides." He wriggled and the light in his eyes danced as he spoke. "Oldest brothers are fun!"

Mr. John looked at Peter and smiled. "I think you are right."

He reached out for Hope's hand, which she took. "What do you hope your oldest brother will be like?" he asked.

Not missing the play on her name, she smiled briefly. "I hope he will be kind and want to read to me. Peter says he is, but Peter has never met him."

"Is that what Peter says?" asked Mr. John.

She looked at Peter and nodded. "Yes, when he is not worrying about us."

"Well, someone had to make sure we stayed together," Peter said quickly. He directed his next words to Mr. John. "How will we know he is our older brother? We've never seen him. I've only read his letters and heard stories people tell about him and I don't believe half of what I've heard."

Mr. John saw the wariness in Peter's eyes. "You will recognize his voice," he said. A slow smile grew on his face. "He's just around the corner. We will soon find out."

He led them on with Timothy on his hip, Hope in hand, and Peter on guard, two steps behind.

Peter felt his heart rate increasing, but kept his breathing normal so he wouldn't frighten Hope or Timmy. They were his only family. He scanned his surroundings again. He was constantly scanning so he could anticipate the need to protect them, defend them, or flee with them if danger presented itself. He'd had to do just that more than once and Peter was taking no chances with this meeting.

Peter's oldest brother was significantly older than Peter. He'd left home and gone to another country on a dangerous mission before Peter, Hope, and Timmy were born. All Peter knew about his brother came from stories told by family friends or were contained in a package of letters he received when both their parents died, leaving Peter to fend for Hope and Timmy in the state's Foster Care system.

The letters were addressed to Peter, having been written after his birth. They contained encouragement and repeating messages of, "I am sorry that I am away," "I know your situation and am helping you from here," "I will come back to you as soon as I can," and "Until I return, you must keep our family together."

Peter never really believed his brother knew what was happening to them and he had little faith that his brother would return, but for some reason, the admonition to "Keep our family together" struck home. Like an anchor, flukes buried deep in the sea floor, keeps a ship in one spot in spite of wind and tide, the admonition kept Peter of one mind when the Foster Care System tried to farm out Hope and Timmy to different families. His dogged insistence that they keep the family together finally won out over the expediency of the system.

Two weeks ago, Mr. John knocked on the door of their foster home and told them their oldest brother had returned and would re-establish himself as their guardian. When the details were settled, Mr. John would come and lead them to him.

That was how they came to be approaching a corner in a hallway that reminded Peter of an airport jetway. The hallway was narrow and well-lit and the floor slightly inclined. A carpet running up the center quieted their footfalls. Turning the corner, Peter saw an open door 40 feet away. Through the doorway he could see several people and was again reminded of an airport and the lounges where you walked into the building from the plane through the crowd of passengers waiting to board.

A man's voice called over the background noise of the crowd. "Is Timmy here yet?"

"That's my oldest brother!" Timmy shouted and pushed himself off Mr. John's hip, landed on both feet, and ran towards the door.

"Timmy!" Peter shouted, but Timmy was through the door. Peter saw two forearms and hands reach out, grab Timmy under the armpits, and move upward in one swift motion. Timmy's feet followed the arms up and disappeared behind the top frame of the door.

Peter grabbed Hope's hand from Mr. John and led her through the door while scanning the crowd and the room for danger.

The room did look like an airport waiting lounge; big, wide, tall, well-lit, with windows across one wall, but the furniture was sofas, wing chairs, and floor lamps, not plastic benches and narrow counters. The crowd looked at Peter and Hope as if they were the ones they were waiting for. Peter scanned the room for Timmy, locating him quickly. He was piggy-back on a trim, fit, and obviously happy older man. The man galloped in a circle, stopped, swung Timmy to his front, gave him a hug, kissed the top of his head, and sat down on a sofa.

"Timmy, I need a rest," he said. "Go meet the others."

Timmy ran off telling everyone that his oldest brother had given him a piggy-back ride.

The man looked up, glanced at Peter, and then focused on Hope. He patted the place beside him on the sofa.

"Come join me," he said. The fun he had enjoyed with Timmy showed in his eyes. His face was as soft and as gentle as his invitation. Hope let go of Peter's hand, walked to the couch, and sat next to the man. They looked into each other's eyes and examined their faces.

"Do you recognize me?" he asked.

"You are just like Peter told me," Hope said. "You are my oldest brother."

The man smiled, put his arm around her and pulled her close. Hope snuggled into the hug and appeared as cozy as newborn mice in a nest made of wool and cotton balls.

"I sure am," he said, "and I am here to stay. Now the only thing missing is a good book." Hope burrowed in deeper and smiled.

Peter heard Timmy happily running about and saw Hope melt.

After a minute, the man apologized to Hope. "Excuse me honey, but I have to meet your older brother." He unwrapped his arm from around Hope, got up, and stood in front of Peter.

They stared at each other, taking each other's measure. Peter was wary and on guard, the man open and defenseless.

The man stuck out his hand to Peter and said, "You kept our family together. Thank you!"

Peter raised his hand to accept the handshake, but the man's hand slide past Peter's wrist and clamped onto his forearm, like two victorious

Centurions acknowledging each other after a desperate battle. The locking of their arms and the squeezing of their hands conveyed in touch the "I love you," that warriors for centuries have been unable to say in words.

"I am sorry I was away so long," he said quietly.

Peter looked at the man, the sensation of the grip stirring his emotions. "You really are him, aren't you? You really came back."

"Yes, I am and yes, I did," he replied. "I am here and won't ever leave again."

Peter felt it go; the wall, the wariness, the defensiveness, and the doubt. It left like snow melting off a roof. First drops of water, then a growing rivulet, and finally the entire blanket letting go, sliding down the roof, cascading over the edge, and smashing onto the ground below, leaving behind a glistening roof reflecting the sun.

"My oldest brother," he said quietly. Timmy, Hope and he were safe. He leaned into the man and placed his head on the man's shoulder.

The man put his arms around Peter and Peter's relief overwhelmed him.

Peter began to cry.

Walter F. Curran

A CONVERSATION

Picture if you will, a two-story beach bungalow, shingles, once white, now a faded gray. Two loose gutters, flapping in the wind like a seagull over a scrap of bread. Stark windows, peering out at the growing seas. Perched at the top of a dune, the sand bleeding away from the step, creating a jump from the porch. Busy during the summer, lonely and sad in the off season.

From the widow's walk you can see for miles but you can also see, right below, a peeling blue dory, pulled high on the sand but still exposed to any passing heavy weather. A dory that once saw loving care but of late, naught but hard use.

This is a house with memories. Of the former mistress, the heart and soul of the house and the grandson who loved the dory. This is a house with a spirit, actually two, forever linked in memories.

"I miss them. They are only here in July and August, not even the full summer. I miss the joyfulness. Blissful ecstasy as they shriek in fun. Days spent on the beach, splashing in the waves or soaking up the sun's rays or out in you, dory, riding those same waves. Endless smiles embody life, even when they don't appreciate it. How precious it is. I long to wrap them in the security of my walls. Set a porch-light for the elders socializing downtown, while I watch over the children, secure behind my locked doors against the evils of the world."

"I miss them too, especially the curly-haired boy. His name was Billy. He reminds me of me."

"I could tell. Whenever he rode in you, I watched you fly through the water."

"I wouldn't go fast when his big brother made him sit in the bow, facing the waves, no matter how hard he pulled on the oars. Billy was frightened and I was mad. The brother cursed, called me a clunker. The day he made Billy cry, I rocked, and he fell out. Every time he tried to climb back in, I'd move away. He swam to shore, and I let the waves take me and Billy into the beach. He never frightened Billy again, nor ever got back in me again. Since then, Billy rowed alone. When he got in, he patted the thwart and I felt good. I got lonely when he pulled me ashore and walked down the beach. I wish I could see him now."

"Wishes are for living people. We are what we are."

"Do you roam through the house?"

"No, I am the house. The house is me, just as you are the dory."

"I like it when they launch me into the surf, but only when they're wearing life jackets. No matter how many times I will them to put theirs on, they don't listen. They think they're smarter than me."

"How can they possibly know what we know? They haven't died, yet."

"It's quiet."

"Yes, without them, the silence is a pall. Oh, there's the wind. It never stops except in the wee small hours of the morning. I often wondered if that's when it is praying. Do you think the wind prays?"

"I don't know. You know so much more than I. You've been here a lot longer. It'll take a hurricane to finish you. I'm falling apart from neglect."

"Yes, it probably will, but we're not finished yet."

"Was it fear that made you leave the house? Fear of drowning? Did you try to return when the water rose?"

"The water never reached above my knees but my chest reached the water. I was only twenty feet away when I fell down. The wind refused to let me up, but I crawled, gasping and got to the porch. I went upstairs when the water lapped at the bottom of the window sills. So strange, surviving outside only to slip and fall down the stairs."

Later, I was calm, looking up from the floor, awash in sand and sea water, knowing I was strong enough to survive the storm, the different I. The new owner talks about tearing me down. Maybe it should be over. For a time, I longed for it to end, yet, I remain."

"At least you had a long time with her. I didn't. If the oar hadn't hit Billy in the head, he could have swum to shore. Six short years together and a five-foot wave made me turn turtle. I still think it's unfair."

"You're young and don't yet understand, life and death are unfair."

Her windows rattled as if she shivered. The wind shook her to the foundations. "Our new owners, fair-weather friends, have once again, left for the safety of wherever they go. It's coming. We've seen too many of these storms. All hurt, damaged, depleted us. Yet, here we are. Even our friend, the tree, leans in anticipation, knowing the struggle to stay rooted is yet to come."

He remained silent, oarlocks twisting in the wind, sand blasting his weathered paint.

"Will Old Glory survive? See how he stands to attention, rigid in the wind. They left so fast after the warning, they forget to fold him and put him on the table in his favorite corner where he can look out the window and see the sunrise. Oh, how he loves to see the sun rise. There was a time when Old Glory was a great symbol of our nation. Now they mock him. I listen and watch when they have that television thing on. It's sad. People no longer have respect for each other. So much has changed, yet, for us, nothing changes. We remain, trapped in this nether world. I wonder, will my journey end if the house is destroyed? Will yours if the dory blows away?"

"I'm afraid."

"No, don't be afraid. Whatever happens, it is fated. It is useless to be afraid. What can we lose that we have not already lost?"

"What do we do, then?"

"We wait, as we always do. Me in the widow's walk, you astride the center thwart and watch the ocean." Puzzled, she asked, "Do you feel the wind? Does it tug at you or pass through you? I feel it when the house moves, siding and shingles fly away. It hurts, like someone pulled my hair."

"I see the wind. In the swirling of the clouds, the ripples and waves, the crestfallen foam, the bending of tree branches, blowing sand. I see it all through soulful eyes, but I don't feel it. I feel nothing."

"Ah. We are different. I feel things."

"You're older. Maybe when I'm as old as you, I will feel things."

"You show your innocence. You will never be as old as I am. We do not age, we simply…continue."

She sighed, a creaking of the boards and lattices. "I do so wish they had drawn you up further on the shore, even behind the house, so I could protect you from the ravages of the wind and waves. If you get blown away or destroyed, I'll have no one to talk to. Alone, as I was the first forty years."

Left once again to face our fate, we wait. For the fury, the rage of nature to arrive and batter us.

June Forte

LESSON UNLEARNED

"There you go," Mary Jo said, as she pulled the zipper of Katie's multicolored parka to the top of its track. "Toasty warm all the way to school." She handed Katie her mittens.

"Mrs. Costello said I can be an angel in the Christmas play, just like you were in first grade Mom. You and Daddy just love Mrs. Costello, too, don't you?"

"We do, we certainly do." Mary Jo tied today's favorite scarf around Katie's neck, and pulled its edge up over her daughter's nose.

Katie pulled the edge of the scarf away from her mouth. "She's the best teacher in the school—in the world, even."

"That she is, sweetie. Now hurry or you'll miss the bus." Mary Jo twirled Katie around, and with a loving push sent her in the direction of the kitchen door.

Hand on the doorknob, Katie looked back. She gave a muffled, "Bye, Mom," closed the door, and danced into the swirling snow.

From the window over the sink, Mary Jo could see Katie at the bus stop deep in animated conversation, her breath turning to vapor. She was hopping from one foot to the other, her backpack bobbing, her hands moving as if she were directing a choir. The semicircle of students seemed eager to hear whatever "Miss Chatterbox" was sharing.

Mary Jo lingered at the sink, washing the few breakfast dishes they had used until the bus had come and gone. It was just Katie and her this week. Ron wasn't due home until Friday night. While she missed Ron, she loved having Katie all to herself for a while.

Later that morning, she sat at the table sipping coffee from Ron's mug. Katie had picked it out at Walmart, and presented it with great fanfare to him on Father's Day. Mary Jo traced her index finger over the word Daddy printed diagonally across the heart on the mug. It brought to mind different snowfall years ago, and a much different Daddy. Despite the warmth of the coffee, she shivered.

"Mary Jo, you piece of shit, get in here now," her daddy was hollering through the hole in the storm door where the window should have been. His voice was thick with drink, his bare belly pushed out from under a much-too-short tee shirt. He opened the door with such force it smashed into the side of the trailer. He staggered one foot after the other, out onto the slippery metal platform where his legs bridged over Mary Jo, as she cowered in her hiding place beneath the stairs. Wet snow fell on his gut and melted into trickles of water that dripped through the grating onto her upturned face. She blinked, and held her breath.

He raised the bottle and drained the beer into his mouth.

"Mary Jo, damn you! Get in here now," he yelled, edging farther out to where the stairs led to the yard. She watched as he lost his footing. He landed on his back. Still gripping the neck of the broken bottle in his right hand, his left reached for the railing, then stopped short. In the silence that followed, his eyes met Mary Jo's through the grate.

"No, Daddy, please."

He tossed the remains of the bottle into the yard and rolled over on his stomach. "You little." Thrusting his arm under the stairs, he rooted his fingers in her hair, and yanked her out. He tossed her through the trailer door as easily as if she were the morning newspaper. "I'll learn you to mind me."

"Don't learn me," she sobbed. "I'm sorry, Daddy. Please, please don't," she cried, trying to merge her body with the wall she had rolled against.

"I'll show you what for." Spittle foamed at the corner of his mouth as he dug under his stomach for the leather belt. He released the buckle and pulled the strap free, wrapping it twice around his palm. The buckle dangled toward the floor, its brass catching the light from the lamp on the table.

As if on cue, Mary Jo stopped crying. She scrunched up her face and curled up into the smallest of balls.

"Learn this, you lazy." He held nothing back. He hit her hard. "And this." The belt tore through the thinness of her shirt. "This'll learn you. Good-for-nothin' trash, just like your mama. This," he spat. The belt sliced her leg. "Will." The buckle jerked a chunk of flesh from her arm that shielded her head. "Learn." He gritted his teeth. The final blow laid her flat. "You." He finished with a kick to her limp body.

She didn't know how long she had been there, lying on the cold linoleum. It didn't much matter. By the time she struggled to her feet, his mood had changed. He was slumped into the sofa, one leg draped over the side.

"Go on like a big girl, Mary Jo, and clean up the bathroom, like I told you before." With a wave of the bottle, he dismissed her and guzzled a mouthful beer before turning back to the television.

Days later, in one of his rages, he locked her out of the trailer in the freezing rain. The lady from the trailer court office called Social Services. They came and took her away. She never saw her daddy again, and she never asked why. It was enough to be warm and to eat, and not to be beaten.

The Nolans took her home the first week in December. They were her ticket to a normal life. A loving couple, they embraced her as a daughter, and she thrived. Although she didn't know it at the time, she was twice blessed when they took her to school and left her in the capable hands of Katie's favorite teacher: Mrs. Costello.

Mom and Pop had done their best to prepare her for school. They didn't understand why she was so frightened.

"You'll love going to school Mary Jo. You'll make lots of friends there," they agreed.

On her first day at school, the Nolans and Mary Jo arrived early. Mrs. Costello met them at the door to her classroom.

"Go ahead home," Mrs. Costello said, assuring the Nolans as she shooed them down the hall. "Mary Jo and I will be just fine."

Mrs. Costello steered her into the empty classroom.

"Here's where you'll sit," she said, showing her to a desk in the front of the room.

Mary Jo sat down and looked around the room. There was a Christmas tree with ornaments and lights in the corner by the window. Red and green paper chains edged the chalkboard, and sets of angel wings filled a box next to Mrs. Costello's desk.

"We're getting ready for the Christmas play, and we're short an angel. I think you would make a wonderful angel, don't you?"

Mary Jo shrugged.

Mrs. Costello walked to the chalkboard and picked up the wooden pointer. "We haven't much time before the play. I'll help you learn your lines, and there are some songs to learn as well," she said, pointing at Mary Jo, who looked up in terror at Mrs. Costello.

"Please don't learn me, I'll be good," she whimpered. "Please, please, don't learn me."

Frank E. Hopkins

DELIVERING DESSERTS

The most fun I have had at the beach is participating in Rehoboth Beach group-house parties. The happy guests smile and talk, the drinks flow, the food is irresistible, and people form new relationships. To receive invitations, a beach house has to reciprocate. We held our party on the first Saturday night in August 2014. The invitations displayed the theme of the party: "Wine and Desserts." Two topics, which we knew would attract guests. Every house member had to perform a task. I had volunteered to buy desserts at Costco in Beltsville, Maryland.

Since I am addicted, most of the desserts on the shopping list had a chocolate component, including: chocolate mousse cake, chocolate fudge cake, chocolate cookies, brownies, milk chocolate crepes, and chocolate cheesecake. My experience giving chocolate candies to women convinced me they shared my passion. But several women in the house, having experienced my one track sweet mind, encouraged, or ordered me, "Get non-chocolate desserts, or else."

"I will, if I can find them."

"Perhaps we should get someone else to bring the desserts," our house leader Margaret announced.

My heart trembled at her words, expecting multiple trays of cut watermelon, cantaloupe, bowls of blueberries and strawberries, supplemented with tasteless pound cake, and a plate full of chocolate-chip cookies. Not my favorite choices.

Concerned with my non-response, she added, "John, if you don't, you'll sleep in your car since all the beds will be taken."

"Okay, I'll buy non-chocolate desserts." I didn't know which frightened me more—sleeping in the car in eighty-plus degree heat, or not having chocolate at the party.

Margaret turned to Paula, "Do you think we can trust him?"

"I'm not sure, but if he had a girlfriend he'd have no problem selecting desserts to please everyone."

As a senior partner in a CPA firm in Washington, I received respect from my peers and staff. The women at the beach treated me differently since my girlfriend left me. Norma and I slept together every summer weekend at the beach for five years. Last February she told me, "I want a permanent relationship."

"You have one. I'm only seeing you. We spend at least four nights a week together."

"John, I want to make it legal and get married!"

Still remembering being divorced and falling into poverty fifteen years ago, convinced I shouldn't remarry in my mid-fifties, I replied, "I'm not ready. Let's wait." Wrong answer.

Norma stormed out of my apartment, refused to answer phone calls, deleted my Friend relationship on Facebook, and blocked her AOL account from receiving my emails. I didn't see her until June at a beach house party. Norma had a thin balding man on her arm—the exact opposite of my former body and ample hair—whom she smiled at more sensuously than she ever had at me. She told me at the party she had lost twenty pounds by dieting. Heartache and loneliness caused my similar weight loss

This would be the first beach house party where Norma did not help me select the non-chocolate desserts and drive together in her spacious silver Toyota RAV4.

Since my task didn't involve cooking, I thought it would be easy. Wrong. I drove to Costco on Friday afternoon at 1:00 to buy the desserts. My car had two large coolers. To keep the desserts fresh, I relied on a quick trip to the beach in my air-conditioned ancient blue convertible, with over 225,000 miles on the odometer.

It took fifteen minutes to load the shopping cart with the chocolate desserts on the original list. Perusing the desserts in Costco, I added a

New York style cheesecake, mango cheesecake, variety pack cheesecake, carrot cake, lemon flower tarts, peanut butter cookies, butter pecan cookies, and rich raspberry crumb bars. Satisfied this dessert cache would please Margaret, I went to check out.

The aroma of the chocolate desserts, the attractive designs on the frosted cakes, and loading the cart had made me hungry. When I walked past a table offering fresh cut watermelon and cantaloupe, I couldn't resist. It had been years since I had eaten this fruit. The first bite of the cantaloupe surprised me; it tasted sweet and its chilled temperature refreshed me. The watermelon had the same impact. I placed two containers of each fruit in the cart.

While loading my car, I ran out of cooler space, leaving most of the items I assumed more heat tolerant in two corrugated cardboard boxes on the passenger-side floor under the air-conditioning vent. I felt safe placing the other items, including tarts, cookies, and crumb bars, on the back seat. Confident my selections would get our party rave reviews, I started out driving southeast on the Washington, D.C., beltway.

The car ran perfectly as I drove on Route 50 over the Chesapeake Bay Bridge and turned left on the two-lane congested Route 404 toward Rehoboth Beach. The air-conditioned car with the internal temperature at 65 degrees had problems fifty yards after the turn. It stalled, and I guided it to a stop on the shoulder of the road. The car didn't start. Driving to the beach must change the personality of competitive Washingtonians. Less than two minutes later, a couple stopped behind me. A man walked to my car and asked, "What's the matter?"

"The car won't start. The battery must be dead."

"I'll give you a jump. Let me park my car in front of yours so the cables will reach."

We attached jumper cables, and the car started without trouble. He removed the cables, and said, "The battery is still low. Turn off your auxiliary equipment including headlights, AC, and the sound system to reduce power usage."

Following his advice, I broke the law by not having headlights on for the trip on Route 404. I hoped I could get to Rehoboth in an hour before the food in the 95-degree heat had turned rancid. I lowered the windows so air blew over me and the food, and prevented me from dying from heat stroke. The pastoral view of ripening corn and green soy beans on either side of the road tempered my fear of breaking down again. The car worked fine for the next fifteen miles as I drove on the Denton bypass and returned to the two-lane 404. After several uneventful miles, the car stalled fifty yards before southbound Route 313. I parked on the shoulder to restart it. Failure!

Not worried, I called AAA at 3:00 p.m. They told me it might take forty-five minutes for the tow truck to arrive. Since it was over 90 degrees, I sat in my car hoping the shade would cool me. However, listening to the cars wiz by at over sixty miles per hour, I became concerned for my safety, worried that one could swerve off the road and hit the car. The hot, humid air exhausted me as I stood five feet from the car. I sweated and waited.

After an hour, I became nervous. At an hour and a half, ready to panic as the interior car temperature rose even with the windows open, two female tennis-playing friends stopped behind me.

I walked to their car, "John, I told you to get a new car the last time you were late for tennis. What's wrong?" Joan said.

"The battery is dead. Can you give me a jump?"

"Do you have cables?" Ann, the passenger asked.

"Yes, they're mandatory in a car with over 200,000 miles."

They drove their car in front of mine, attached the cables, and the car started.

As I removed the cables, Joan said, "Good luck, we're on our way."

"Can you follow me, in case, the car stalls? The problem might be a faulty alternator not charging the battery."

The car stopped after fifteen feet. "Must be the alternator," Joan said. "You'll need a tow."

"I know I called AAA two hours ago, and they haven't arrived."

"Well, we need to go. Good luck," Ann said.

"Are you going to our party on Saturday?" I said.

"Yes, we wouldn't miss it." Joan answered.

"Then you can help make it a success. The desserts are in the car. If they're not delivered, there'll be no party."

"Our car is almost full. Let me look at them," Joan said. She and Ann walked to my car.

I opened the coolers and said, "These are the critical desserts. If they get warm, we can't use them." They gazed lovingly at the chilled fruit, chocolate mousse, two chocolate fudge cakes, and five assorted flavored cheesecakes, and other delicacies.

"We can take the two coolers."

Feeling relieved, I said, "Thanks," and waved as they drove away.

My euphoria vanished after five minutes when I realized I still had other desserts in the car. Panicking, I redialed AAA and explained my predicament. They countered, by saying, "We sent someone there an hour ago. They couldn't find an old blue convertible with a black top and Maryland plates."

"I haven't moved since 3:00. They couldn't miss me. Can you send someone else?"

"We'll try. It might take up to at least an hour during rush hour."

A half hour later, Betty, an old friend, a member of a different beach house, stopped behind me in her red Miata sports car. She said, "John, you need a new car. How many times has it broken down in Washington?"

Embarrassed and lying, I said, "Too many times. I'm getting a new one next week."

"Can I give you a ride?"

"No, I can't abandon the car here. But you can help me by taking some desserts to my beach house for tomorrow night's party."

"Okay, but I can't leave you here, and my car won't hold much."

"I'll be okay. I've called AAA." But I didn't tell her they failed to show up for the first call.

The two cardboard boxes fit on her passenger-side floorboards and seat, but she had filled the rest of the car with luggage.

With only tarts, cookies, and crumb bars left, I felt better, but still concerned about AAA.

A half hour later, Norma pulled up behind me. She asked, "What's the matter?"

I explained, ending my monologue by saying, "Baked goods are all I have left. Would you like a cookie?"

"They probably have peanuts. Still trying to kill me. If your car didn't do it, you're now using another ploy."

Her smile told me she wasn't serious, but I had forgotten her deadly allergy to peanuts. Since she wouldn't eat them, I didn't ask her to carry them to the beach house, afraid they'd never arrive. After saying goodbye, I ate one peanut butter cookie to satisfy my hunger pangs. It tasted so good I had six more, which I washed down with bottled water.

Two hours later, the sun set and the bugs came out. Still no AAA response, what should I do? Stay outside and get bitten by mosquitoes and maybe develop malaria, or sit in the car and get crushed by a swerving chicken truck?

As I slapped my arm to kill a bug, a man drove into his driveway next to my car. He asked, "What's the matter?" in a pleasant relaxed manner.

I told him a summarized version of the afternoon events, including the AAA no shows.

He smiled and said, "What instructions did you give AAA?"

I said, "My disabled car is on the corner of Route 404 and 313."

"Typical mistake. Happens all the time. You should have said Route 404 and 313 South. There is a 313 North, on the Denton bypass. AAA assumed it was that location. Call them back."

He listened, while I called, "John Willard here. I called earlier, but gave incorrect instructions."

Before I could continue, the AAA man said, "We've sent two trucks. Hope you're not playing a joke on us. We know your name and address and may send you a bill for the two missed pickups."

Fearful, I might spend the night alone on the dangerous Route 404 I gave him the correct address. He said, "If this is a trick, I'll send the police to arrest you." My problems delivering desserts had escalated to potential incarceration.

My savior motioned for me to hand him the phone. I did. He identified himself, verified my mistake, and laughing, handed me the phone. The AAA representative had hung up.

The tow truck arrived less than an hour later, and we drove to Rehoboth Beach.

"Where do you want me to take the car?" the driver in his young twenties asked.

"Rehoboth Auto Repair on Route 1 in Rehoboth," I said.

Tension drained from my body as he nodded his head and said, "Okay."

I looked forward to sleep when I reached our beach house after an exhausting day of standing around waiting to get the desserts delivered and my car towed. "After you drop the car off, can you drive me to my beach house?"

"Yeah. I'll need directions when we get to Rehoboth."

After I transferred the remaining desserts to the tow truck he dropped me off at the Oak Avenue house. I expected a barrage of questions from Margaret and Paula.

When I walked in with the baked goods, and placed them in the pantry they rushed from the back porch, smiled, and shouted, "John!" They gave me a friendly hug.

"John, your dessert selection is perfect," Margaret said.

"I couldn't have done better myself," Paula responded.

"Thanks for putting them away. We didn't get here until 8:00 and thought you forgot us until we looked in the fridge and the pantry. You must have arrived earlier and left for dinner after storing them," Margaret responded.

"We'll never question your judgment again." Paula said.

Since I expected a different welcome, I remained silent.

"John, I'd like you to meet Judy. She's my guest this weekend. We've told her all about you, your great career, and what a nice guy you are," Margaret said.

Bewildered. Were these the same women who last week threatened to make me sleep in my car? Judy, whom I had noticed sitting quietly in a chair, bounded to the floor.

"Hi John, Margaret said you're a good tennis player. I'm looking to reclaim my game. She said, 'If you asked nicely, John would help.'"

This bundle of energy revived this tired man without a car. "How can I refuse that invitation?" I noticed her blonde hair, slim body, blue eyes, infectious smile, and effervescent personality. We talked for fifteen minutes. She told me of her transfer from her firm's Chicago office to Washington, and her hobbies. When I decided she was perfect for me, and would like me as long as she believed I delivered miracle desserts, I had to call my female rescuers. Joan answered first.

"Thanks for putting away the desserts. How did you get in?"

"No one answered when we rang, so we looked for a key. Found it above the door sill in twenty seconds. You should lock your house. There may be mass murderers in Rehoboth."

"Can you do me a favor?"

"What?"

"Not mention you delivered the desserts."

"What's in it for me?"

"A weekend on my sailboat, for you, Ann, and two friends."

"When?" Joan asked.

Since I knew I had her, I replied, "Any weekend after Labor Day when it's cooler."

"Sold. How long must we stay quiet?"

"Two weeks. Is Ann there?

"Yes, she heard our conversation, and shook her head yes."

Ten minutes later, Betty agreed to my scheme, ending our conversation with "Why?"

When I introduced her to Judy at the party, she smiled. After Judy went to get a glass of wine, Betty said, "Now I understand."

Once Judy returned, Ann walked over, introduced herself and in a jovial tone asked, "Judy, do you like to sail?"

Women make the best matchmakers and give great advice. I purchased a silver 2014 Lexus convertible five days after the party.

Sarah McGregor

HE LOVES ME KNOT (excerpt)

Chapter One

A blast of blaring horns and electric guitar explodes into the still-dark morning. Heart racing, I fling out an arm to shut off the clock radio. Giving myself only a second, I throw back the covers and scuttle for the dresser. It's cold as hell and my head is throbbing from too much wine. But like most unpleasant things, waking is best done quickly.

I grab the riding breeches and shirt I set out last night and head for the kitchen. Yanking open the oven, I turn it on broil, simultaneously flicking on the coffeemaker and aiming the remote at the TV. I'm a gunslinger in a bad western, attacking every available appliance within firing range. As I hover in front of the oven's weak warmth, the coffee sputters away like an old man with prostate problems. God, I hate getting up.

"*Chester County can expect a high of forty-one with intermittent precipitation and a raw wind out of the west.*" The perky weather lady delivers the forecast as if announcing a cure for cancer. Tossing an empty wine bottle into the recycle bin, I flip her the bird and head back into the bedroom for warmer socks.

And happy effing birthday to me. I'm forty today. I fumble in the drawer, pulling out a bra and an ace bandage before latching onto the soft wool of my knee socks. And—what the hell? I flip on the lamp to see what I've unearthed. It's a knot of hair. I'd cut it off when I was a teenager—a big snarl I'd saved as a kind of commemoration of my first kiss, my first love. Nick—the *only* love, if you want to split hairs, pun intended. It must have fallen out of the drawstring bag I've carted around with me for ages. Containing assorted treasures including Mom's sorority pin, the hospital wristband from my tonsillectomy, and my plaster handprint from kindergarten—given to and returned by my unsentimental parents—I can never quite bring myself to toss it. I stare at the palm-sized snarl. Momentarily dumbfounded, I'm not sure whether to laugh or cry.

After all these years, a weird little relic of who I used to be. Back when I thought life was simple. When I was naïve enough to think I would define it by the choices I made. I was so wrong. Instead, decisions and fate twist and turn back on each other until it's impossible to see how things first went awry or how to even begin straightening them out. Reflecting back on the tangle of stupid choices I've made, on the times I let others dictate them for me, I know it's like this knot.

With a start I come back to myself. Darting a glance at the clock, I throw the wad of hair in the drawer and hurry back to the kitchen. One thing I've learned, *reflecting* doesn't help.

* * *

Two hours later, I survey the group of horses and riders milling around the stable yard. From atop a restlessly pawing gelding, I wait with the others for the foxhunt to begin, my mount notably less patient than the others.

"What's she riding *this* time?" Ellen's comment carries over the din.

I take a drag off my cigarette. I don't need to hear my name to know I'm the topic *du jour.*

"Seriously, Diana." Bob stops his horse near mine. "That horse looks like trouble. Is he yours?"

"*No*, he's not mine. Rusty has him in on consignment. He's paying me to try him out. He'll be fine," I add as the horse pins his ears at Bob's mare.

Bob laughs. "Yeah, right."

"I heard one of Rusty's horses went over backward with a girl," Ellen says, maintaining a safe distance. "Broke her neck. His name isn't Zeus, is it?"

Great! Right now, I want to break *Ellen's* neck. And while I'm at it that son of a bitch Rusty's. I should know better than to trust a horse dealer, but I'd be the last to admit it to these two. Besides, a girl's gotta eat.

"This is Napoleon," I lie.

"Napoleon! Looks like you're the one about to meet her Waterloo." Bob brays at his stupid joke just as my gelding lashes out with a nasty kick. Ellen snickers and starts singing that Abba song, *Waterloo.*

As if their company alone isn't annoying enough.

I move the horse away, hunching my shoulders against the stiff wind. Not daring to take my hands off the reins, I bend forward to grab the cigarette and flick it to the muddy ground. A nagging sense of dread roils in my stomach with this morning's coffee. And now, to make matters worse, I have that damn Abba song stuck in my head.

Twenty years ago, I felt blessed to get paid for doing what I loved— riding horses, especially the tough ones. Now it seems stupid. What kind of fool advertises a specialty in training horses with *issues*— crazy, rogue horses? I've racked up more broken bones than an NFL linebacker. Without the big fat paycheck to make up for it. In my next life I'll come up with an easier way to make a living. Right now? Bob's right. This horse is a ticking time bomb. I regret bringing him here. I regret getting on him. And I regret that now I'm too stubborn to get off. I blow out a breath and scratch the miserable beast on the neck. Hopefully Son of Satan, or whatever his real name is, will settle down once we get going.

Or not. Twenty minutes out and his rough coat is lathered in sweat, his teeth grinding in agitation. Another fifteen and he's pulling on the reins so hard I'm sure my arms will be ripped from their sockets. Everything rattles him. The yipping hounds moving in a sea of waving tails, the sharp blasts of the hunting horns ... and galloping in a group with other horses? It's the equine version of that movie *Speed;* I'm riding the runaway, about-to-blow bus through innocent commuter traffic.

On the first check, the hounds have trouble regaining the fox's scent. Impatiently jigging in agitated circles, I wait near the other field members at the edge of a thickly wooded covert. In the woods, the yips of eager hounds blend discordantly with the sharp calls of the staff. It echoes back to us in an eerie cacophony that sets the hairs on the back of my neck prickling. Beneath me, the gelding stiffens.

Occasionally, I catch a glimpse of a hound's white feathering tail through the trees. Another breaks covert only to turn back and restart his search. When the doubling of the hunt master's horn signals they've found the line, the chorus of baying hounds escalates to a fevered pitch, and my horse's head flags up in terror. He's going to bolt and I ready myself. When instead he rears up, I'm taken off guard. Instinctively I curl forward, clutching my arms around his lathered neck. We teeter there precariously, all eyes drawn to our drama, and Ellen's warning comes back to me with stark clarity.

Finally, the big horse comes down, landing with a jarring thud that nearly sends me somersaulting over his shoulder. He leaps forward and I barely manage to right myself as I fumble for the reins. I consider an emergency dismount, the equestrian equivalent of abandoning ship, but can't do it. Stubborn and pigheaded to the end, apparently.

The gelding gains speed, his muscles bunching and firing so rapidly I lose the cycle of strides. My vision blurs with tears, a frenzied kaleidoscope of gray sky and the rusts and golds of autumn leaves as we veer onto a winding path through the woods. Branches tear at my face and arms. Until I hit a tree. Dead on, to use a bad pun. An abrupt, shocking impact accompanied by the sudden and total cessation of sound. Of life.

From a distance, I'm aware of all this. And of floating. I drift for hours, and for less than a second. Not enough time to catch myself, but more than enough to contemplate an entire forty years of life.

Chapter Two

Dilaudid is a fantastic drug. I had my first taste of it in the ER. I'd come off a young horse with a bad habit of bucking, and after a long wait and some x-rays, my arm was pronounced broken. I think they had to put pins in it. Whatever, what I remember is the IV drip. The instant that powerful painkiller entered my system, I went from excruciating agony to floating. Floating on a fluffy cloud of blissful euphoria.

Now, as I lie here and regain conscious thought, I feel it again. That rush, like heavenly narcotics flooding my veins. No pain. Even the shame and regret I've carried for decades like some kind of sinner's hair shirt fade to insignificance. *Heaven.*

Gradually I become aware of my earthly surroundings. Sunlight, warm on my face. A breeze gently moves a strand of hair across my cheek, and the earth is solid and comforting against my back. Like an orchestra adding each section until all play together in concert, I hear birds in the distance, and closer, a horse munching grass. The metal bit jangles as he chews and casually shakes a fly from his neck. I have no urge to open my eyes and confirm my impressions. Even when I detect the sound of distant hoofbeats moving toward me at speed, I lie still, relishing my very existence.

Hmm, two, possibly more, sets of hooves. Unfortunately, the intruders don't share the appreciation for serenity that my equine companion and I do. My horse picks up on their tension and moves restlessly, as if debating whether to stay or shy away.

"She's here!" A man's voice.

"Is she ..." Another man.

"Fetch the horse, Henley," the first man says. "Go to the house and send for the physician." His efficient recitation of orders settles the man he called Henley, who soon canters away with *my* horse. Someone dismounts to approach me.

"Stanhope, if you can manage here I'll go advise the group to continue without us." The third rider, silent until now, has reached my side and grunts in agreement. Sufficient reassurance for the mounted man, apparently. He, too, canters off. By my hazy calculations, only the man called Stanhope remains.

Again, I consider sitting up, opening my eyes. But I don't. At the moment, all my energy is focused on what I'm hearing—posh British accents. Who *are* these people? *I say, lovely day here in La La Land, what?* A giggle that comes out more a snort escapes my mouth.

Stanhope speaks, perhaps in an effort to comfort me. That's the effect, anyway. His voice, that accent, flows over me like silken sheets— luxurious and sultry. In my soporific state, I'm transported off on a sensual tangent, only vaguely registering the content of his words. It's like a voluptuous dream attracting me like a magnet or … warmth. I'm totally enveloped in the sensation. *That must have been one hell of a knock on the head.* I haven't felt anything like this for … well, a long time.

My rescuer touches me and my lips curve into a smile. He feels for a pulse, I think. And I must have one because he showers me with praise. I couldn't be more proud. His fingers move to my head, gently sifting through my hair and then down the back of my neck. A tickle of shivers chases down my spine. *Heaven.* I should be a cat. Purring seems appropriate.

Thoughts of my ex pop unwelcome into my head. We butted heads a lot before I learned the futility of it. Inevitably at some point in any argument, Cricket, my otherwise faithful companion, would trot over to him, *the enemy,* and roll onto her back, legs spread like some cheap whore. Gloating eyes never leaving mine, Jimmy would crouch down and rub the dog's belly. Never missing a beat in his harangue, he demonstrated his power over me and everything I held dear.

But now, as Stanhope's beautiful voice and hands caress my body, I forgive that little dog. This man could well be as big an ass as my ex. But as long as he keeps his hands on me the point is moot.

"Nothing broken here." Stanhope moves down my body to slip off my boots and I pray the examination will be thorough and long-lasting. His glorious hands meticulously probe each ankle before pushing my skirt aside to continue up one leg.

Skirt? Since when do I wear a skirt? And with enough material to sail a small boat. As he gently traverses his way toward my knee, I cease to care. The tongue of my inner dog lolls blissfully out the side of my mouth.

"Don't like your color," he says. I can tell without looking he's frowning.

Crap. Let's focus on the stuff I'm doing right. Remember my pulse?

"Steady." Resettling himself near my shoulder, he unbuttons my jacket. "Poor gel, it's a wonder you can breathe at all. Have to cut it open."

He rambles on about the *damned* this and the *bloody* that as he rustles around in his pockets. What the hell has his boxers in such a bunch? It's a sports bra. That shouldn't be too terribly shocking. And why is this man, who doesn't sound remotely close to AARP eligibility, referring to me as a *girl*?

The sound of rending material is followed immediately by a great gushing wave of air rushing into my lungs. Like reverse drowning, oxygen floods my system leaving me writhing and gasping for control of it. A low moan raises the hairs on the back of my neck until I recognize the source as my own mouth. To make matters worse, Stanhope has ceased his reassuring soliloquy. I mourn the loss of it along with my delightful floating state, apparently nothing more than a boring case of oxygen deprivation.

"Bloody hell!" Unlike his earlier murmurs, he's practically shouting.

He soon quiets, but his tone is agitated. And I confess, between that and the oxygen tsunami, so am I. He proceeds to adjust and readjust my clothing, mumbling, cursing, and sometimes even chuckling as he does. His hands, steady and firm until now, are clumsy with nerves. Am I bleeding to death? Surely that wouldn't inspire amusement. What the eff? I try to ask but no words come out, just more of the disconcerting moaning.

"Now the jacket. Maybe just these two buttons." The sound of a horse cantering toward us causes his to nicker. "Mulgrave," he calls out. "Just in time."

The rider comes to a halt. "Returned as fast as I could. What—"

"Fine! Everything in place." Stanhope straightens my jacket. "Nasty bump on her head. Otherwise, she's endowed, erm, equipped with, uh, good health."

I hear Mulgrave dismounting. "Problem?"

"Just help me get her up on my horse." As he speaks, Stanhope gently gathers me in his arms, easily lifting me as if I weigh nothing.

I'm absolutely no help in the venture. I dangle limply over his arms like some life-sized rag doll. Nevertheless, he handles the whole procedure quite gracefully, passing me to Mulgrave, then taking me back once he's mounted. Soon I'm settled comfortably against Stanhope's big warm body, rocking gently with the even cadence of his horse's gait.

We walk for a few minutes before Mulgrave breaks the silence. "So?"

"So?" Stanhope's voice vibrates against my ear on his chest.

"You're blushing."

"Don't be an ass." Stanhope clears his throat. "Let's cut through the Hobson property. Easier terrain."

"Agreed. I'd feel better if she was conscious by now. You?"

Stanhope shifts me in his arms and I can practically feel their eyes on me.

"As would I. For the most part," he adds under his breath.

"What the hell does that mean?"

I may be flopping along like some worthless sack of grain, but I'm wondering the very same thing. I mean, I was right there and I haven't a clue what Stanhope's problem is.

"Nothing!" he answers, tension thrumming through his body.

"Really?"

"I checked the young lady for injury," Stanhope says after a moment.

"Makes sense." A few more moments pass, during which I assume Mulgrave has stared his friend into submission.

"Fine!" Stanhope says, finally. "If you must know, I became concerned with her color. Pulse was steady enough, but she was pale and—"

"*And* get to the point."

"I deduced her stays were the culprit. I used my knife to cut them open. I was perhaps a bit overzealous because, well, the entire corset split. Ripped right in two, by God!" Stanhope shifts me in his arms. "I simply wasn't prepared for the extent of the, uh, bondage."

What the hell? With my ear pressed against his chest, I'm the first to detect the low rumble of a chuckle. He tries to disguise it behind a cough but soon he surrenders to an all-out guffaw, his whole body shaking with it.

"I know it's ridiculous, Charles," he says, when he manages to get himself under control. "But I meant only to loosen the thing, not … Well, it was more than I planned for."

"That's *it*?" Now Mulgrave is laughing. "Shaken by a pair of tits?"

Suddenly grasping this tangle of a discussion, I thank God for preserving my mostly unconscious state. It's the next best thing to sinking permanently into the ground. This has to rank as the most mortifying experience I have ever, *sort of,* been a party to. I may not have the biggest rack in the world, but no one's ever actually laughed out loud at them. The only redeeming part of this whole debacle is the men's insistence on referring to me as a *girl*. I may have the chest of one but my face has definitely seen the far side of thirty. Either their eyesight is extremely poor or these guys are masters of sarcasm.

"Charles, enough! She'll come around. I don't wish to cause embarrassment." *Too late for that!* "As I said, they … *it* just took me by surprise."

"Indeed!"

"I trust you won't gape at the girl or her, uh, *neck,* when next you encounter them—*her*!"

"Of course, I won't." Mulgrave chuckles. "I suppose it *would* have been rather awkward if she'd come to right at that moment."

"I can only imagine the look on my face." And then under his breath, Stanhope murmurs. "Christ, the finest French courtesan would kill for such an exemplary pair."

"What's that?"

What the …! I heard that even if Mulgrave didn't.

"I said, who are her people? I don't believe we've met." And again under his breath. "I would have remembered."

"Diana Burton," Mulgrave says. "A guest at Grace Manor. Lady Byrne will chaperone her for the season. Daughter of an old friend apparently. Not surprised you haven't noticed her. One of those chits straight from the schoolroom. All downcast eyes in pink and frills."

Lady who? Schoolroom? Frills? I have no idea what they're talking about.

"God save me," Stanhope says.

"Lucky no one came upon you." Charles is laughing again. "We might even now be planning your nuptials."

"Charles?"

"Eh?"

"Do shut up."

Charles chuckles but changes the topic, the conversation only occasionally interrupting the steady rhythm of the horses' hooves. I pay no attention. I'm completely baffled, my blissful oblivion a thing of the past. Who *are* these people? Why are they talking like the goddamn royal family? And how could Stanhope possibly describe my chest as *exemplary?* What kind of man marvels at a chest that more resembles a piece of plywood than the proverbial pair of ripe melons? My thoughts ricochet from one possibility to another. None are particularly viable until I hit on the only thing that makes sense.

I'm *dreaming*.

Obviously knocked unconscious in the fall, I'm having an especially vivid, perhaps narcotics-induced, dream. *Duh!* The earth shifts back into its properly orbiting and rotating position. I relax, resolving to lie back and enjoy the ride, literally and figuratively.

As soon as I reach this conclusion I feel the horses pick up their pace, signaling we near our destination. Leave it to me to dream up realistic horses that anxiously perk up for the promise of clean stalls and fresh hay. The mood is contagious and I experience the first compulsion to open my eyes. The flurry of agitated fluttering that ensues does nothing but create a nauseating strobe-light effect. I change tack and try to sit up. Which definitely does *not* help. I envision my fantasy dream heading south as I vomit all over the hero, and slump back into my rag-doll heap.

A voice calls out. One turns into two and then more as we're surrounded by the pandemonium of heated discussion. The horse shifts nervously, and I'm unable to separate the swirling impressions until I feel Stanhope lean over. Belatedly, I recognize his intention to deliver me into the hands of the forming mob. Quite frankly, the prospect of being lowered into shark-infested waters could not be more terrifying. In a blind panic, I claw desperately at his jacket.

My puny efforts go unnoticed as for the second time that day I sink into blackness.

Chapter Three

"Such a lovely gel, isn't she, Dr. Jackson?" A woman's voice whispers near my ear and this time I successfully manage to open my eyes. There she is, curly gray hair, rosy round cheeks, and vivid blue eyes peering down at me from about two inches away. I press back into the pillow and cautiously take in my surroundings. Overhead, an expanse of apple green material forms a gently draping canopy. Velvet roping gathers matching curtains to drape elegantly at the corners of the huge tester bed I'm lying on. Definitely *not* a hospital. The dream is still on.

The woman motions to someone and an older bald man appears. He scowls down at me through a pair of wire-rimmed glasses.

"How many digits?" he asks, holding up three fingers. He has the same British accent as Mrs. Smiley and my Man Posse. These two are no hunky Stanhope, but the tones are still soothing. I relax into the soft down of the pillow. "Can you speak, gel?"

Oh! A response is expected. Odd for a dream, but I swallow and tentatively clear my throat. "Three fingers." My voice is scratchy from disuse but both he and the woman seem pleased.

Nowhere *near* as pleased as me! I've got the accent, too. I sound like I'm straight out of effing *Downton Abbey*. With use and a few medicinal sips of brandy, my voice settles into a low, sultry timbre, like warm honey. I concentrate intently on the ensuing questions, hoping they require expansive essay responses. Unfortunately, I don't know the lady's name, what day it is, or where I am, but I make damn sure to use as many words as possible to convey it. The lady seems genuinely upset by my poor performance so I nix the idea of requesting a book for an interlude of oral recitation.

After much grunting and scowling, Dr. Jackson pronounces his verdict—rest in a darkened room, minimal stimulation. Ironically, this sets the woman, Lady Byrne, he calls her, into a flurry of activity. Curtains are drawn, pillows fluffed and my lady's maid, Kate, is summoned. *Lady's maid!* Maybe I died and this is heaven because it's way too good even for a dream. I watch spellbound as a diminutive redhead, complete with mobcap and apron, scurries into the room. Like a scrappy little sheepdog, she quickly gains control of the situation. Within minutes she's herding the older pair from the room.

"I'm so happy to meet, er, *see* you," I blurt out when we're alone.

"Poor Miss." She pats my hand comfortingly. "What can I get you?"

"Well … I could use the bathroom." I've been trying to ignore it. Everyone knows peeing is a surefire way to end a dream.

She eyes me quizzically. "A bath?"

"Eventually, I suppose. Right now, I need the ladies' room."

"Lady Byrne's?"

Huh? "The toilet."

"Uh, toilette?" The little maid gestures helplessly toward a dressing table.

"I have to *pee*."

"Well, Saint Bride's bloodshot eyeballs, why didn't ye say so? Let me help ye to the pot. Can ye stand or shall I bring it to you?"

Pot is better than *toilet?* Whatever. I will *not* be using a bedpan. I assure the girl I'm okay to walk and she helps me shuffle around the bed to a large silk-covered screen. *God, am I sore.* Now that I'm upright, my head is pounding and my ankle feels like it's on fire. Surely a dream supplying a personal maid and a British accent should leave out physical discomfort, but … the gift horse's mouth and all that.

I don't know what I expected. All the *rest* of the furnishings look like something straight out of a period piece on public television so I should have been forewarned. But when we round the screen, instead of finding the door to the bathroom, there is its historically accurate alternative—I'm shocked. I stare dumbly at the commode. Complete with arms and an upholstered back, the chair has a round hole in the seat with a ceramic pot placed fittingly below. Thankfully, Kate leaves me alone to do my business. After searching in vain for some way of flushing, I emerge from behind the screen. Since I didn't wake up, did I just wet the bed back in the real world?

Over the next half hour, rather than heeding the prescribed period of quiet, Kate keeps up a constant chatter. Almost as an aside she mentions my age. I miss most of what she says after that because... *eighteen years old!* I look down at my hands. Actually *look* at them. Gone are the calloused and bony middle-aged versions I'm used to. These babies are beautiful, soft and elegantly long-fingered with pearly tapered nails. Surreptitiously I pull up one sleeve of my voluminous white nightgown to run a finger up the smooth, pale skin of my arm. Heading north, I trace the pliant flesh around my eyes, lips and throat. I look up to find Kate staring at me. *Oops!*

"What is it, Miss? Does yer neck hurt?"

"Oh, no, no. I just, erm, have an itch." Sending a silent apology to my beautiful skin, I turn my besotted caress into a good, hearty scratch. The repercussions of this are mammoth. I've gained a *lot* of experience along the bumpy road of life. Sure, I've made mistakes. But I can learn from them. Probably. The point is, I'm a wise old crone housed in the body of a youthful siren. Seriously, the British accent is now mere icing on the cake.

I take stock of the cards I've been dealt in this weird dream game. *Young body, check. Seasoned mind, check. Historical setting, check.* Kate returns and with minimal prompting I learn that I'm an only child and heiress to the estate of my parents who recently perished in a carriage accident. *Orphan, check. Money, check.* My new guardian is my uncle. From Kate's scowl I conclude Uncle Horace is not a favorite of hers. She tells me she was hired by my ailing Aunt Mary, my father's sister, to attend me in my London season. This, I gather, is something like stud season for thoroughbred mares. When well-bred girls are old enough, they're trotted out for inspection by eligible males, then married off to the highest bidder. That's the abridged version, but I think I've grasped the main idea.

"Yer color's better," Kate announces as she folds a blanket. "This wee rest has done ye wonders. Suppose ye could eat somethin'?"

"Thank you, Kate, but might a bath be arranged?" *I love this accent!*

Within minutes, a line of uniformed men toting buckets of steaming water and a copper tub file through the door. Kate, with an armload of towels and assorted fancy glass bottles, follows the procession, joined soon after by Lady Byrne.

"Diana!" the lady exclaims as she clears the doorway. "Fancy a bath, do you? Oh, your color *is* better. Surely Dr. Jackson can't object. *And* that handsome Lord Stanhope has asked to pay his respects later." She giggles. "He'll be relieved to see you alert and speaking."

Technically, *I'm* not doing much speaking. Who could with these two in the room? I am curious to see what my mystery rescuer looks like, though. Will he live up to his sexy voice? Lady Byrne shoos the footmen out of the room, flapping her arms like a mother goose chasing goslings. I'm left with the tub and Kate, who will apparently assist.

"Here we go, then." In one swift motion Kate grabs two handfuls of material and whips the gown over my head. *Whoa!* I cough up a strangled little squeak and scramble into the water—*youch!*—which is much warmer than anticipated. With my hands on either side of the tub I slow my descent and as I do, I get a gander at my new lower half. *Holy shit!* My hands aren't the only things new and improved. Dream Diana is hot. And I am *not* referring to water temperature.

Kate hums a little tune as she drizzles the contents of one of her bottles onto a sponge. She kneels down next to the tub and I want to object. I could really use some alone time right now. My protest dies a quick death as the warm pressure of the sponge kneads firmly into the tight muscles of my shoulders. Privacy might be overrated.

L. L. Powell

IN THE NEW BRIDGE'S SHADOW

I had tried to tell my granddaughter Lizzie that I did not want to go with her, couldn't care less, wasn't interested. I argued with her on the phone for a full twenty minutes, knowing all the while that she was still coming to get me by the sounds of her driving in the background of our conversation. I hustled as fast as my 86-year-old frame would move, to change out of my farm clothes into something suitable for a Sunday drive.

It wasn't a Sunday; it was a Wednesday, but you would not know it for all the traffic on Dover Bridge Road. I could see it from my porch, as I sat squeaking out a rhythm in my cane rocker, waiting for her little blue SUV to race up my dirt lane, dust billowing in her wake. The traffic was headed one place, Dover Bridge, the new one that is. They had officially opened it today, and everyone wanted to be one of the first cars to cross it. The Governor and his wife had taken the ceremonial last drive across the old bridge, then the first official drive across the new bridge, in a 1941 Buick convertible. It had been all over the midday news. I guess they could not find a vintage car from the year the old Dover Bridge was opened to use.

I had been one of the first ones to cross the old one when it was new in 1932, sort of. We share the same birthday, myself and the first Dover Bridge. The morning of the opening ceremony my parents and some of their friends packed picnics and piled into the back of an old Ford Model TT farm truck. It had wooden slats for the bed and rails.

My mother was sure that the bumpy ride on those rough, splintery boards, in the back of that truck, had been what had sent her into labor.

Finding a nice spot on the bank, they joined the other picnickers who had gathered to enjoy the spectacle of the ribbon cutting. This new bridge was going to be a godsend, an inter-county connector that would cut a two to three-hour ride to get emergency medical help down to twenty or thirty minutes. Most of the neighbors from the surrounding area had put on their Sunday finest, and come down to the edge of Choptank River in Caroline or Talbot County to witness the opening. Boats were crossing back and forth through the opened center span, just for the novelty of the experience.

My father had wanted to be an engineer when he was younger, but there was no money for him to continue his education beyond the sixth grade, when he had to quit to help on the family farm. He had become obsessed with any structure made of steel, and the new bridge was no exception. My mother told me that for the handful of years it took the McLean Company to raise that bridge out of the muddy marsh, father was down there at the construction site at least once a week, watching or chatting with the workers.

That day was supposed to be a day of celebration. Father was in the middle of telling all who would listen about how the bridge was 843 feet long, 24 feet wide, with a 16-foot clearance and a one-of-a-kind "Warren Truss Swing Bridge." He was in his glory, lecturing on his favorite topic for a rapt audience.

"Warren Truss bridges are generally for railroad crossings, so that makes it unique that they are using it here for this bridge. There are two other swing bridges in Maryland, but we've got the only one with Warren-style trusses. Do you see the steel girder triangles? Those are equilaterals, and that design makes it strong and lightweight at the same time. As cars and trucks drive across it, the force from their weight will be channeled into the beams, spreading out, and become a shared load across the bridge surface. In the center there, in that housing just above the waterline, is a great big mechanism that will make the bridge swing open. When a boat pulls up to it, the keeper will throw a switch that will make the center turn, opening it for the boat to pass through. Then he'll close it back up."

He did not get to really launch into a full oratory on the history of Maryland bridges, because I chose that moment to throw the switch on my own bridge mechanism, sending my mother into labor.

My mother's water had broken on the Caroline side of the Choptank, and the hospital at that time was housed in the upper floors of the Tidewater Hotel in Easton, on the Talbot side of the river. There was only one way to get there in time, and that was to cross the new Dover Bridge.

Poor mother was unceremoniously loaded back into the bed of the truck once more, as our friends and neighbors helped her to try and get comfortable on the blankets they had just been picnicking on. The men climbed into the cab of the truck and the women all sat in the back with her, just in case mother would deliver during the trip. The center span of the bridge was open at this moment, as all the local dignitaries were having their picture taken with the giant scissors and ribbon for the local paper.

The state trooper keeping order at the proceedings flagged father down, ordering him to stop and turn around until he heard my mother moaning from the bed. It was the trooper that made the officials move and close the bridge, long enough to let us pass, as they did not want to at first. They went on to have their ceremony after we had crossed, but the excitement of my birth was strategically left out of the history of Dover Bridge.

The happy barking of my black lab, Dulcie, brought me out of reminiscing. It was Lizzie, tearing up the drive.

"Pop!" She jumped out of the driver seat, waving at me, barely getting it in park.

"Hey there, Lizzie girl!" I'll never tell the others but she's my favorite, reminds me of my Margaret, all red curls, coltish limbs, infectious mirth, and joyful spirit.

"I see you changed your clothes, I thought you said that doing this was just nonsense."

"Hmph, smart ass." She had me and she knew it.

"Do you want to drive?"

"That newfangled foreign thing? No. Besides, your mother would kill you if she knew you let me drive."

My license had been taken by my daughter a while ago. It was one thing for me to drive around the farm in my old beater pickup, checking the herds and the fence line, but I was not supposed to be out on the roads anymore. I had failed to adjust to just how fast things go these days out on the roads, and it terrified Lizzie's mom, the thought of me driving 40 miles an hour, everywhere I wanted to go.

"Well, let's go! This is going to be so cool!" She snapped her seatbelt on, and I did the same.

"Bunch of nonsense, old bridge worked just fine." It still bugged me that they had built a new one.

"Pop! Seriously. The old bridge is falling apart. There are big holes in the deck. In the summer it gets so hot that it sticks open, and they have to have the fire companies come to hose it down to cool it off, and just a couple years ago they opened it during the winter and it froze that way for three days."

"All things that could have been fixed, but these days it's easier to just waste a ton of money getting something bigger and fancier." I was irritated by the whole thing. That bridge meant something to me, but I didn't expect her to understand.

"Pop, you cannot tell me that sitting by the marsh, when it's hot and stinky, because the bridge is stuck open and you can't cross, is better than driving up above it."

She had me there, the marsh around the bridge, when the tide is out, has a smell that is overpowering with decay and rotting vegetation, When the wind is just right, that marsh funk mixes with the eye-watering fragrance from Porter's pig farm, where it wafts from the bend of the river, just north of the bridge, choking and gagging those unlucky enough to be stuck in one of the bridge traffic jams.

"Look, we're not the only ones that had the same idea, Pop!" We were part of a long convoy of cars and trucks, all passing through the little crossroads called Bethlehem, headed for the bridge.

"Just think, Pop, next summer the old bridge is going to be open as a fishing pier. We can take a picnic out there and sit in the shade of the new bridge and fish. If we sit on the Talbot side, we'll be able to see that cool sailboat relief they put on one of the big concrete supports."

I didn't answer her, thinking about the sight of something that had served shore folk for eighty-six long years being turned into a fishing pier. Maybe I was having hurt feelings because the bridge and I were the same age and I had watched my own usefulness shrink and fall away.

"Look, Pop! Oh my gosh, here we go! This is so exciting!" She was bouncing in her seat and I could not help but smile over her joy at something so simple as crossing a brand new bridge. My father would have loved Lizzie.

The view caught me by surprise. I had never seen the river from this vantage point, usually reserved for the osprey that nested on the trusses of the old bridge, summer after summer. It was unlike anything I had ever seen outside of a *National Geographic* pictorial. The river stretched out in twists and snarls, like a great copperhead tangle in the sun. The marsh on the Caroline side oozed lazily away from the banks, forming great patches of varying shades of green marsh grasses, scrub, and the white blooms of the rose mallow.

"It's beautiful." I didn't realize I had said it until Lizzie responded.

"I know, it's gorgeous! It makes me feel bad for calling it stinky."

I couldn't help it, I laughed, and soon we were both laughing like loons, as we coasted down the other side, into Talbot County.

"Let's go get ice cream, Lizzie, and then we'll come back across it, and enjoy that view from the other direction."

"Okay, Pops!" She floored it, making me smile. Watching her as she chattered on about what had happened at school that day, I found myself thinking about the old bridge, wondering if it looked at the new bridge, watching it grow up, piece by piece, knowing that its shadow would soon eclipse it and felt proud, knowing that it had earned the right to rest and enjoy watching the new generation carry on.

* * *

The cracked vinyl booth of the ice cream parlor pinched Lizzie's leg, eliciting a squeal from her that turned heads. I took my time, not wanting to repeat her mistake on my good church pants. I didn't try to hide my excitement any more from Lizzie, as we tucked into our hot fudge sundaes.

"I wish I had brought that camera your mother gave me for Christmas last year. The view is amazing from up there. Your Grandmother Maggie would have loved to paint it."

"Right? I mean the view from the Sharptown bridge is cool, but our bridge's view has got character. Who knew that marshes could be so pretty when you see them from above?" She put down her spoon, a serious look replacing the normal jovial one on her face.

"Pop?"

"What is it, Lizzie girl?"

"Mom said you were born the same day that they opened the old Dover bridge. That's pretty cool. You've never told me that story. Will you tell me now?"

I was speechless and choked up all at once. My stories had stopped being requested by my grandchildren and great-grandchildren, years ago. I had to take a moment to try and not let her see the tears that had come unbidden to my eyes at her simple request.

"Pop? I'm sorry, you don't have to tell me if you don't want to. We can just finish our ice cream and go back. If we time it right, maybe we can catch the sunset. There is a shoulder on the bridge now, so maybe we can even stop for a minute and get a longer look."

Composed now, I looked at her sweet young face, so full of worry that she had upset me. So much like her Grandmother. "No, it's okay. I want to tell you about it."

"Really? Cool." She put her spoon down and was completely focused on me.

Right then, I felt like the old bridge, we were brothers at that moment, looking at the face of the new bridge and I smiled.

"Your great grandfather loved bridges. He had wanted to build things, great big things made out of steel, but there was no money for him to keep going to school after the sixth grade, so he never got the chance. When word came that they were finally going to put a bridge across the Choptank, it was like a dream come true for him....

Russell Reece

THE WHOPPER

My mom and I liked going to Rehoboth Beach, the place with the boardwalk and all the fun, but my dad liked to fish, so most of our beach days we drove down from Philadelphia right past the turn off to Rehoboth to one of the fishing beaches between Dewey and the Indian River Bridge.

That day in the late summer of 1985 was no exception. Around two in the afternoon we pulled into the sandy parking lot where a handful of cars were clustered around the entrance to the path over the dune.

"Not too crowded," Dad said.

That was a good thing because Dad would get upset if there were a lot of people on the beach who weren't fishing. "They can swim anywhere they want," he would say. "There are only a handful of places where we can fish."

We unpacked the car. Mom and I carried a couple of bags and each took handle of the cooler. Dad had the umbrella, his chair and fishing stuff. We used to have to take more than one trip, but I was almost ten now and could carry as much as Mom. We headed up the path between the snow fences, our feet squeaking through the dry sand. Before we got to the top of the dune I heard the waves pounding. It was a sound I also felt in my tummy and it was one of the things I loved about the ocean. And then there it was—the beach spread out in front of us, the waves coming in, and sunlight sparkling on the water.

There was a group of people who weren't fishing and several others to the south who were. Dad led us north, past the swimmers and sunbathers. It looked like he was going to keep going until Mom called out, "This is far enough, Bill. Any further and you're going to have to carry me."

Mom had worn her pink and white checked bathing suit under her clothes. She took off her blouse, stepped out of her shorts and stuffed them into a beach tote. While she and Dad spread the blanket and set up the umbrella, I took off my shirt, ran down to the water and splashed into the shallows. The waves were pretty high and crashing down. I wondered how much swimming I'd be able to do. The water was cool and I loved the way the sand washed out from under my feet as the wave rolled back into the ocean, loved the way the water hissed into the sand and left foamy bubbles. I scooped up a handful, tasted the salt and remembered the last time I was here, tumbling through a churning wave, sand and saltwater up my nose and down my throat.

Dad brought his chair and fishing gear to the edge of the wet sand. He took off his Phillies t-shirt and tightened the waistband string in his baggy orange bathing suit. "Come on, Charlie. Let's take a quick dip before I get started."

"Okay!"

We waded in, turning sideways to the first wave. When it hit, Dad made a face and gritted his teeth. "Cold!" he said. He pushed past the spot where the waves were breaking and dove into the smoother water behind. When he surfaced he was up to his chest. "Come on, don't be a wimp," he said.

I worked my way through the crashing waves and finally made it out to him. We splashed around for a while, treaded water, and rode the swells up and down. Then we floated on our backs. My ears were under and I could barely hear anything. I looked up at the clouds; felt the water lifting me and it was like I was drifting away in outer space. I could have stayed like that all day but after a few minutes Dad was ready to go in. "Okay, sport. I need to catch some fish. We'll come back out in a little while."

We headed back to the shore. Mom was sitting in Dad's chair wearing her floppy hat, her arms wrapped around her knees. I waved and then got bowled over and rolled onto the sand.

"Are you okay?" Mom was up heading my way.

I laughed and scooped up a handful of water to wash the sand from my face. "Why don't you come in? It's really nice out here."

"Too rough for me," Mom said. She turned to Dad. "It looks like we're going to have the beach to ourselves this afternoon." The swimmers and sunbathers had picked up their blankets and umbrellas and were heading over the dune. Two fishermen remained on the beach but they were far south of us.

"That works for me," Dad said. He took a piece of bait out of his small cooler and was threading it onto his hook. "I've got a feeling. Today's the day I get the big one."

Dad said that every time we came here. If he caught anything it was usually small or some kind of junk fish he threw back. Mom looked at me with a smirk and rolled her eyes.

"Yeah, I got a feeling," Dad said again. He winked at me, picked up the rod, walked to the edge of the water and cast the line. The bait-rig with the triangle sinker soared through the air and splashed far out into the water. "Get ready, Charlie. It's gonna happen."

Dad walked back to his chair and set his rod in the holder. He reeled a little so the line was tight and then sat down, his hands behind his head, his eyes focused on the rod tip.

"Let me know when you catch that whopper," Mom said. "I've got a book waiting for me under the umbrella."

"It won't be long," Dad said.

Mom went back, sat on the blanket and pulled out her book.

I took a walk up the beach looking for shells or anything interesting I could find. When I turned around I was surprised how far I had gotten. I jogged back, weaving in and out of the surf, trying to stay in a few inches of water so my feet splashed all the way. Some seagulls had landed and they lifted up as I came toward them, hovered over me, and then landed again after I passed by.

Over the next couple of hours Dad and I went for another swim and Mom and I played Frisbee. Dad caught a little sand shark and I held it as he took the hook out. I could feel its muscles when it tried to wiggle, and its skin wasn't slippery like other fish I'd held; it was

55

more like sandpaper. I waited for a wave to come in and let it go in the shallow water. Dad checked the rig and cast it out again.

I went and sat under the umbrella with Mom. One of the other fishermen was lugging his stuff up the dune. That left only Dad and one other guy far down the beach from us. "That shark was pretty cool," I said to Mom.

She flipped the page of the magazine she was looking at. "Well, at least your daddy caught something today."

"Think we can stop at the boardwalk on the way back?"

"I'm sure we can, as long as your dad's not too tired from all the hard fishing." She nodded in his direction and smiled. Dad had fallen asleep in his chair.

Two ladies had come over the dune and were walking toward the beach. They were older than Mom. One had curly dark hair. The other was a blonde and a little shorter. Mom doesn't like me to call people fat, so I'll just say they were pretty big ladies. Both wore shorts and tank-tops and neither had any bags or a blanket or anything.

When they got to the water the dark haired lady kicked off her shoes and waded in. A wave crashed and she ran away from it as water surrounded her up to her knees. She laughed and splashed the water with her hand. She motioned for the blonde to join her, but she shook her head. The dark haired lady ran back in like a kid would do. It was funny.

"You want something to drink, honey?"

I looked back at Mom. "Do you have any root-beer?"

She dug in the cooler, pulled out a can and as she handed it to me her gaze fixed on something behind me. Her mouth opened and her eyes got big. I turned around. The dark haired lady had taken off her top and was stepping out of her shorts. It was too far away to hear what they were saying but the blonde seemed to be trying to stop her. She had her hand up to her mouth and was nervously looking around. The dark haired lady threw her shorts down and ran toward the water. Her white underwear glowed in the sun and it made me think of a snowman with legs. The blonde looked at us, shook her head and mouthed the words, "I'm sorry."

Mom was staring at the women like she couldn't believe what was happening. "She's just wearing underwear," I said. "Can she do that?"

Mom smiled at me but it didn't seem real. "No big deal, honey. Her underwear covers more than most bathing suits do."

I thought about that for a second. There were a lot of girls with tiny bathing suits down at the boardwalk. I looked back. A wave washed over the woman. She wiped the water from her face and motioned to her friend to join her.

"You don't need to watch," Mom said. She reached into her beach-bag, pulled out my new Spiderman comic and offered it to me. "Why don't we both sit here and read for a while." Her gaze shifted back to the women and her eyes grew large again.

I turned around. The lady had run back onto the beach and was trying to pull her friend into the water. She was screaming and the dark haired woman was laughing. She finally ran back in by herself, pushed through the first wave and dove into the still water. She started swimming on her stomach, kicking her feet, her face in the water, her arms doing the swimmers crawl. Her big white bottom bobbed up and glistened in the sun.

"Okay. We're going," Mom said. She got up and started piling things into the beach-bags. She yelled at Dad. "Bill!"

He didn't move.

"Go wake up your father and tell him it's time to leave."

"Aw, Mom."

"Go on now. We'll stop at the boardwalk. Quickly!"

The woman was floating on her back and drifting in the calm water. Her friend was sitting in the sand, the clothes folded on her lap. When I got to Dad he wasn't asleep. He was staring ahead, not at the woman but a little off to the side, and giggling to himself. When he saw me he tried to stop but just then the woman spit a stream of water high into the air and Dad laughed so loud I thought he was going to choke. I'd spit water before and it had never been that funny but watching the big woman floating there, the spout coming up and Dad laughing so hard, I started giggling, too.

I finally told him, "Mom wants to go."

Dad turned and looked at her. Mom was folding the blanket and with an angry expression on her face she said, "Now!"

Dad got up, put his tackle away and folded the chair. The woman was still floating on her back and had drifted close to Dad's line. He shouted, "Hey!" and tried to wave her off. She thought he was waving at her so she smiled and waved back.

"*Bill!*" Mom yelled. "What are you doing?"

Dad looked at Mom but before he could say anything the fishing rod jerked. The woman had drifted over the line and was grabbing at it, trying to lift it over herself. She spun around onto her stomach but instead of getting the line off, she got it hooked under her arm. Dad picked up the rod. When the woman felt the tension on the line she squealed and turned around. She was standing now with water almost up to her neck and waves lifting her up and washing over her. She was trying to get untangled but the line was wrapped around her a couple times.

Dad handed me the rod and waded to the edge of the water. "Pull the end with the sinker and come on in," he yelled.

The woman tugged on the line but couldn't seem to break the sinker out of the sand. She threw up her hands like she was giving up and started to laugh. Dad waded toward her, pushed through the next crashing wave. Mom was standing beside me now, her arms folded, her face fixed in a scowl.

The blonde came up to us. "She's so spontaneous," she said. "I never know what she's going to do next. She's from Arkansas and was so excited seeing the ocean for the first time."

"Don't people in Arkansas wear bathing suits?" Mom said.

"We didn't expect to come. We were in Baltimore. It was a last minute thing."

Dad got to the woman and jerked on the line until the sinker came loose. He held onto the line and they both waded toward shore. The woman's underwear clung to her body and as she got closer I could actually see right through it. I wondered if she realized.

"Oh, God," Mom said under her breath.

The woman made some comment I couldn't hear and Dad laughed. Just then a wave crashed into them and they were knocked down and washed onto the sand. Dad scrambled up, took the lady's arm and tried to help her but she just sat there in a big flabby puddle with water rushing around her, laughing.

I couldn't help but laugh, too.

"It's time to go, Bill," Mom said.

Dad looked at Mom and made a gesture with his open palms that said, "What am I supposed to do?" The lady rolled onto her knees and pushed herself up. Dad unwound the line from her neck and under her arms but it was still hooked somehow on her back. "It's stuck in your clasp," he said.

In a slow, southern accent the woman said, "Just undo it, honey, and take it out." She wrapped her arms across her chest.

"*Don't you dare!*" Mom said. "Cut the line, Bill. Cut the darn line."

Dad looked at Mom like he was hurt. "I don't want to lose my rig," he said.

The woman grinned. "You don't have to worry about losing your *rig*, honey."

The blonde gasped. Dad looked at the big woman for a second and they both laughed again.

"That's it!" Mom said. She snatched the rod from my hand and threw it down on the sand. "You get finished with Miss Eighteen-Hour, you better hightail it to the car or we'll be gone."

"It's Bali," the woman said. She rolled her shoulders around. "Playtex never worked for me."

"Stop that!" the blonde shouted.

"What?" the woman said. She giggled. Dad had the biggest grin I had ever seen.

I had no idea what they were talking about but Mom huffed, grabbed me by the wrist and pulled me away. We picked up our stuff. I had one handle of the cooler and turned to look back.

"Just keep your eyes straight ahead, mister," she said. "You've seen enough today."

"Why are you mad at me?" I said.

"I'm not mad at you."

I was going to ask her why she was mad at all but I've done that before and it didn't work out so well.

Dad got to the car the same time we did. He was running and out of breath, dragging his sinker through the sand several yards behind him. He hadn't taken the time to disassemble his fishing rod. Mom got in and slammed the door. Dad and I packed everything up.

"What's going on?" I asked.

"Not now," he said.

We pulled out of the parking lot and headed toward Rehoboth Beach. No one said anything for several minutes but then Dad started to laugh. Mom stared at him. He looked out the side window and then back to the road. He started laughing again and Mom slugged him on the arm. "It's not funny, Bill."

"Yes it is," he said.

"I don't want some woman prancing around in her underwear in front of my nine-year-old."

That surprised me. "You told me it was better than a swimsuit," I said.

"Oh!" Dad smiled at Mom like he had caught her at something. "Is that what you said?" "I didn't say better," Mom said. "I said it covered things up."

"Then what's the problem?"

Mom lowered her voice and, in a whisper like she thought I couldn't hear, said, "You could see everything. You never know how that could affect a child. Who knows what he's thinking now?"

Dad looked at me in the rearview mirror. "So, Charlie," he said. "What did you think about that lady back there on the beach?"

"Bali?" I said.

Mom put her hand over her mouth.

"Yeah, Bali," Dad said. "Anything bother you about her? Any thoughts you want to share?"

What thoughts did I have? I thought Bali was happy and funny. I wished more people were like that. I liked her southern accent. But I was pretty sure Mom didn't want to hear any of that. We pulled up to a red light and they both turned in their seats and looked at me.

"Well..." I said. "I thought she was a pretty good swimmer."

Mom bit her lip and sat back down in her seat. She shook her head and then her shoulders started to jerk like she was laughing.

"Anything else?" Dad said.

"Nope."

He nodded. "Well, all right then."

POETRY

Shirley Brewer

COWS AND CONES

In my boring childhood, we drove
out to the country to watch cows
munch grass in tedious fields.
On our way home, we stopped

at Meisenzahl's Dairy for grape
ice cream cones: plump
purple scoops, melting sculptures
worthy of a rapid tongue.

Our old Chevy, my parents in front,
my two siblings and me in the back.
Billboards, tumble-down barns,
Burma Shave signs—all gone now.

More than ordinary, the way
a cow and cone afternoon
takes on a warm aura like a pie
fresh from yesterday's oven.

HIGHBALLS

Jim Beam and ginger ale recall
Christmases in upstate New York,
our house a-shimmer in poultry heat,
sprays of fake holly rakishly tucked
behind picture frames—Dad's touch.

Mom and Auntie run the kitchen
like gourmet elves in red and green,
their cooking marathons
fortified with festive highballs
stirred in reindeer tumblers.

Mom raises a toast to the turkey,
a bird she bonds with each holiday,
having stitched it up to hold in the stuffing:
You can't take a sewing needle to something
without making a connection.

Katie Spivey Brewster

BURNING CANDLE

String in
Wax

Match to
String

Flame of
Light

Piercing
Night

Wax
Drips
Down

Smoke
Wafts
Up

Shadow-ceiling
Bouncing
'round

CHEERING THE EAGLE

20 July 1969
I'm pushing open the sliding door—
Stepping out onto the patio,
Looking up into the night sky
I spot the moon.

Can they *really* be on it?
The Apollo Astronauts.

I'm just three weeks shy of my
10th birthday—a whole decade.
NASA has probably been at work on this
Mission for longer than I've been on Earth.

I watched the rocket launch
From Cape Canaveral, Florida,
On TV with my family—
And, now, those guys are *up there*.

Looking back inside the house
I see the fuzzy screen
On my aunt's and uncle's television set.
It's time, it's on!

This is it! It's for *real*—
They're doing it!

I take one more glance up at the moon
Before stepping back through the door
From the patio to the den
Where family is sitting on the edges

Of the couch and chairs,
Eyes glued to the screen,
Jaws dropped, holding our breath—waiting.

Then, it *happens*—
Astronaut Neil Armstrong
Comes out of the Lunar Module,

He backs down the stairs
Onto the surface of our moon
And we're all on our feet . . .

As he steps down—
We jump up.

Carol Casey

THE FIRMAMENT

Above the wind, the stars. Beyond the stars,
the firmament. You know your Latin, so
you know that firmament means something
that strengthens or supports. Metal braces
a garage door, a biscuit binds two planks
of pine. Adept in the material world,
someone creates the brace and makes
that biscuit's thin space. You.
                          The ancients
worshipped their craftsmen gods. Moderns believe
in what we can imagine. Stories we tell.
That's how I can see you sailing silent
into the cove, sail trimmed close.
River lapping on the green shore
where two fawns play, watched by their worried
mother, and you, now telling me this tale
of a quiet sail that in my mind's eye
I see and hear and it takes root. Like
the sycamore seed carried on the wind
over wide water, that finds congenial ground,
unfurling, one small leaf and another.

HOW TO MAKE A BEACH

The glass river invites breaking.
Dive and shattered water heals behind you.

Swallows flee their nests, dip and whirl.
Eagles fall upward, from cliffs into high currents.

On the bay, a tugboat chuffs behind a barge,
the rusty sound of work carried by water.

You think you are floating through life.
You think, I have made nothing.

You stumble out of the river, wet and dripping
like some kind of beach B-movie monster.

In your wake, a tiny ripple
pushes a grain of sand against a pebble.

Kristin Davis

DELICATE THINGS

Pressing toward the stream,
she crashes through a spider web
unseen across the trail,
scowls at the sticky threads
on her face, wipes the strands
on her pants, keeps going.

She slows her pace in the fields,
rolling yellow goldenrod,
dried milkweed, bursts of aster,
discovers a monarch wing,
coppery glow like stained glass
within its mullions, lead-black.

In the feathery tall grass,
a fragment of turtle shell,
mahogany and caramel,
thin like a fingernail,
translucence and darkness
held to the light.

At dusk, an orb-weaver suspends
a lone strand from leaf-tip
to gutter, anchors to ground,
lays a perimeter, places spokes,
spins concentric circles,
all without pause.

She watches. How many laborious
miracles has she thundered through?
How much fragile armor shattered?
Her letter, asking forgiveness, she leaves
in a book, awaiting discovery.

GROWING COLDER

He refuses a cane, takes halting steps
down granite stairs to the lakefront,
slips into a child-size lifejacket,
closest at hand, even though it does not buckle.

Wading, chest-deep, he tips his head back,
closes his eyes, enjoys the blush of sun
on his eyelids, the sensation of floating,
though his bare feet graze the rocks.

His granddaughter, the lifeguard now, watches closely,
fears he is falling asleep, dares not disturb him.
He disturbs easily. Hears intruders at night.
Slips away from the house at perceived slights.

Fireman Emeritus, he has passed the ax on to his grandson
to chop wood for the fire. Like layers of skin, he has shed
other titles: teacher, black-diamond skier, business owner,
Bible-study leader, master of the house. He is thin.

He lives in his son's house in summer, does not decide
when dinner is served or the lawn gets mowed.
The same son who dumped him to the ground once,
jumping from a seesaw. He cannot show the hurt.

This native Mainer now feels the cold. Well before
the first frost, he wraps in wool blankets, scoots closer
to the fire. Months early, he begins packing for Florida,
before ice can form around the edges of the lake.

NO SUCH THING AS SILENCE

For Christine Blasey Ford

This woodland walk is not silent,
breeze tussles boughs, squirrels
stir pine needles, water bugs
scatter wide-rippling circles.

A restless mind carries
the sodden silence of its secrets,
held still, hand over mouth,
radio static, rolling tear.

They say God speaks in a still, small voice,
tuned to silence. What stories are kept
by these moss-muffled stones?
What is the sound of a blossoming flower?

Every silence is expectant.
The hush of seed
under the earth,
under the snow.

Beth Dulin

TINNITUS

The tenant house was cold in winter due to the lack of insulation. So they wrapped it in heavy plastic and installed a wood-burning stove. But she didn't like the idea of sacrificing trees. That was the winter the buzzing in her ears started. She had to ask everyone to repeat what they were saying. Her fears kept multiplying and stacking up around her. She knew she had to change something. So maybe she'd recognize herself again. Before there was no way back into the life she was losing.

HOME

The story I tell myself
is that coming full-circle
and ending up at the start,
a quarter century later—
may be some kind of failure.
But traveling these empty roads,
it seems like the first time
I can recall seeing
the fiery October trees
before they give in
to the slow decay of winter.
The geese arrive,
their nasal, off-key voices,
a lonely reflection
of the dark chill, settling.
Inside, I slow down,
sit for hours watching the fire—
trying to break free and welcome
this inevitable surrender.
But then the uninvited early sundown
has me counting the days until
the light comes back around
to stay a little longer.
And the songbirds begin talking outside,
their voices carried through
the warm, intoxicating breeze
of spring easing into summer.
So, I think—
this must be the place,
after all.

Kari Ann Ebert

THE RESISTANCE OF MEMORY

she stood at the counter
back to window hand on knife
wept over onions chopped for stew
willed the blade to become
shackles to chain her there
her legs granite columns
belied cracks threatened to collapse
as bare feet dug into floorboards
wishing to grow roots in the wood
for fear she'd fly after him again
down the hall out the door
to his car abandoned
in late spring of last year

Irene Fick

THE TENNESSEE WALTZ

I hide behind the kitchen door
stare as Mom and Dad link hands
glide across the den, lost in a lilting song …
I was dancing with my darlin'
to the Tennessee Waltz when an old friend
I happened to see…

Mom's hair jet black, long and silky
a pompadour frames her forehead
her skirt billows over curvy calves.
Dad, stocky and gruff, moves like Astaire,
fingers firm on Mom's back.
They look like movie stars.

… introduced her to my loved one
and while they were dancing,
my friend stole my sweetheart from me.

They dance without a trace
of their daily silences. No crippling words
explode with tobacco smoke.

I am 10 and tired of bearing
the ordinary ache of their misery.

How I wish they would keep waltzing
triple time around and around while holding
on to that moment at midnight, holding
tight to one another so that nothing
would ever be lost.

BLINDSIDED

You're compiling a list for your trip to the mall
or pulling on those new yoga pants. You're moving

the recliner to the corner. Maybe you're paging
through travel brochures, or rushing to your desk

to finish the poem that sliced through last night's
dream. What you don't know is that beneath

the veneer (skin, bones, muscle) another universe
is at work. Sometimes, it announces itself with an ache,

a cough, a thunder in the belly. Most of the time,
it is silent, engrossed in its own cycles. Somewhere

in this universe, a random cell rebels. The poison
comes out of nowhere. It is stealthy. Sooner or later,

it begins to spread, wander with purpose, or without.
You will not know any of this. You will not be disturbed

until much later, perhaps when it's too late. You might
be re-arranging furniture or trying a complicated yoga pose

or planning a week at the shore or writing a poem loaded
with metaphors …

A tornado whips the wind, decimates a bucolic town
on some distant plain. A stranger with a grudge fires

bullets into a crowd. A plane goes down in a different sky.

Elissa Gordon

PHOTOGRAPH

My mother's hand is raised
in a gesture toward her
short dark hair,
a face intent on conversation,
neighbors up from the city for a visit.
Webbed lawn chairs clustered
in a conversational circle
made the vast lawn intimate.

I am the one behind the Kodak Brownie,
taking the picture.
If I'd had a panoramic lens,
you could have seen that
children ran between large maples,
rolled and tumbled down the gentle slope
of the back lawn.
My brother, off in the distance
held a ball,
our father bending to him
in an attitude of instruction.

When I look at this photo,
my eye always goes
straight to my mother.
In all the activity,
her stillness, her ease
is the center for me.

SPANISH MOSS

It starts with the Spanish moss,
not with the thick humid air,
or the hum of mosquitoes,
or the whine of car tires on pavement,
just a mass of threads
in all those shades we name,
the way we do with paint samples,
yes, moss, also heather, lichen, dove gray.

It helped if I looked up at the moss,
kept the tears that formed welled
at my lower lid,
not spilling over onto my cheeks,
tracks crisscrossing each other
like the webbed mass that I dreaded,
dreaded would be dank
or perhaps dry,
frayed and broken down
like the cuffs and collar
of one of my father's old dress shirts,
abandoned somewhere,
fear that loneliness would choke me
until I swayed like the host tree
in the barely there breeze,
enveloped in this reverie
of the South
a final resting place
marked, but remote
and unreachable for me
when I leave.

Marilyn Janus

TWO HAIKU

Cape May-Lewes Ferry

Rough water forecast
Mah-Jongg game in terminal
Winds, Bams, Cracks, Dragons

Brafman Family Dentistry

One giant toothbrush
One plaque-infested molar
Match made in heaven

Melissa Mattie

I AM

Yesterday
I made dinner too early.
You didn't like it. I am such a screw-up.

You spit in my face.
I don't deserve respect. I am unworthy.

You put me in a choke hold.
I deserved it. I am out of line.

I realized everything I do to try and make you happy
isn't good enough. I am a failure.

You peed on me in disgust
while I cried. I am the dirt on the ground.

I tried to get away and leave you.
You took my keys and money. I am a prisoner.

You told me if I ever left you, you would make sure
I was ruined first. I am damaged.

You told me if I get wrinkles like my mom
you wouldn't love me anymore. I am ugly.

You made fun of my job. I told you one day
you would be proud of me. I am unimportant.

You called me horrible names.
I am what you say.

You told me to change my number and not talk,
not even to my mother. I am controlled.

You told me I am not allowed to leave the house.
I am isolated.

You had your way with me even though I cried
and begged you to stop. You said I wasn't allowed to say no.
I am your possession.

You wouldn't let me sleep until you were done
yelling at me. I am tired.
You turned the cold water on and made me
get into the shower. I am humiliated.

You hit me three times across the face.
I am a victim.

Yesterday you held me on the ground
and strangled me. I am going to die.

Today
I am in the hospital while they count my wounds
and take pictures of my body. I am exposed.

I am trying to learn how to live without your control.
I am dependent.

I am hiding from you in a shelter.
I am afraid.

I had a panic attack and was told I had PTSD.
I am diagnosed.

I cried in my sleep.
I am still healing.

Now I am smiling again.
I am hopeful.

I am accepting the truth God says about me.
I am worthy.

I am no longer a victim.
I am a survivor.

The nightmares have subsided.
I am an overcomer.

I am gaining self-esteem.
I am beautiful.

I am providing for myself.
I am independent.

I believe that my mom was right: I am not ruined.
I am stronger.
I am able to let go and forgive you.
I am merciful.

I am leaving the chains behind me.
I am free.

Yesterday, I belonged to you.
Today, God has set me free.
Now, I am His.

Claire McCabe

UNDER THE CLOOTIE TREE

She's only nine, but she's the liar
the bad one
in the family.

Blue bruises, dark circles
under her eyes …
her punishment?

What keeps her up at night—
bad dreams of tigers, things
with stripes like

an uncle's shirt, stinking
of sweat and wine. Still
she'll take pennies, sly,

from a blind beggar's cup,
trade them for sweets,
suck on a candy stick till

pennies and uncles, tigers
and lies bind up together
in sins so tight,

she runs to the Clootie tree
past the deep well,
to untie the tangle,

trade lies for strips, straps for rags,
uncles for stripes, toss in a penny,
and pray for the blind.

Note: A Clootie tree is a part of Celtic tradition carried out for healing. The tree, which grows near a holy well, bears ribbons and rags that have been tied to its branches as prayer offerings.

Nancy McCloy

LOVES ME, LOVES ME NOT

It could be said you broke my heart
one petal at a time; you gave bouquets
when telling lies—they glided off your
tongue as smoothly as skaters waltzing
on ice.

It could be said that purple cosmos
is my favorite flower, legs tall and frilly
like asparagus ferns. They bend easily
in all directions at the slightest breeze—
much like your promises and wandering eyes.

> I cut red roses from my garden
> for you today, wrapped them in iridescent
> tissue and gave them as a gift. Thorns
> pricked your hands when you grabbed
> them with surprise.

It could be said I got revenge today,
one drop of blood at a time.

S. B. Merrow

RETURNING UNDER SAIL

We work the breeze, the patterns
it makes high on a shapely canvas
where smallest flutters tell

of perfect tension, the speed and tack
of our hunger to cross the gravid ocean.

Diamond baubles of sunlight
scatter and dissolve ....

Once more before the wind,
we tumble down emerald peaks on
emptied zephyrs and wallow back

to rest among the shells
where seagulls cluck and pick at kelp,
yellow-legs sticky with gravity—

heavy with legend—fleets of stars
rattle the rigging in our ears

as spinnakered birds sail overhead
half-seen, half-felt, celestial
bodies that pull on a loafing sea

that rises only to meet the moon.

WINTER HARBOR

after the painting "Winter Am Main" by Daniel Sheldon

Is there nothing new
in the drab and dated world,
an obsession, a heist—

a woven thing I could hang
on the hull of my mind,
gilded, effortlessly elegant?

I look out
        at snow falling
on the oblivious sea, clinging

just moments to the branch
where a cardinal calls
his tawny mate, a landscape

where reds show best, like
embers in the early dusk—
and can almost hear

the music of winter's ship,
its sheets coiled and sails furled,
a beaded necklace of sound—

recorders burble below the decks
on the drum of her empty hold, and
I wonder what gesture, dance,

or baroque betrayal
would free my frozen soul
from its mooring.

Russell Reece

HIGH FLYERS

Forgoing dirty business
a dozen buzzards soar aimlessly
against the summer sky.
Circling slowly,
the wide whorl rises
higher with each turn
like smoke up a chimney.
I watch them effortlessly
climb through the vortex,
growing smaller and smaller,
and I am caught
in the rapture, the lifting up,
the cleansing,
the joy of leaving everything
on this blue earth behind.

LEAVING

Even after
the untethering,
the pushing off,
the drifting,
light
from the cabin door,
reaches
across water
black as pitch,
a golden thread
following
wherever I go.

Willie Schatz

MY COUSIN DIED NINE YEARS AGO

which sucks now as much as then

he was—can I write *is* because he still *is-*
was?—my mother's brother's child
guess I cannot say *is* there
cause I gotta get real
and he *really* is
not here physically
but he is
emotionally and spiritually
with his picture on my shelf
and
his voice in my head

shit

I want my cousin to come back
but he did not
after the first year
and no he has not
after the ninth
so maybe just maybe
he won't come back
and fuck that
cause he was more brother
than cousin

yeah I admired him
(except for his worshiping

the fucking Yankees)
with that perfect infielder stance
and being the superstar Under 17
everything at Camp Takajo
and because he helped me
learn to play tennis and baseball
and showed me
how to be
compassionate and caring
by using kind words
when I wanted nasty ones

and yeah
I loved him
though I never said
those words
while we were growing up
because boys do not say
I love you
to each other
until way later
if they say it at all

shit

I wish I had told him
when I had the chance
because I do not remember
whether I told him later
so I have to settle
for kissing the top of his head
maybe ten days
before that
horrible despicable
sucks-ass disease

took him to wherever he is
which is somewhere else
but not here

Catherine R. Seeley

EIRE

High above the cliffs of Moher,
At Dingle and at Slea Head,
Up in Sligo, Benbulben's glen,
In Clonmacnois along the Shannon,
My disposition turns mendicant
Begging earth, wind, sun, and sea
To so fill the coffers of my senses
With the memories of their drama
That such visions will never be spent
And I shall be spared the parting.

Terri Simon

BODY BLOWS

Grief lives in the body, and so I move.
If I curl in on myself, fetal and frozen,
muscles lock, tighten, until my lungs
forget their job, I fossilize.
If I rush back to the world, words
are a sandstorm, stinging me blind.
Each death connects to every other,
like sinews and ligaments, stretched, snapping.
Slow movement eases the pain,
small wounds bind over time.
I move. To do otherwise is to die.

Peggy Warfield

SUMMER GUESTS, 2016

Summer guests have gone
Morning light streams
Through library windows
Warmth of the family still
A shawl around my shoulders

Hear the laughter of two-year-old Emerson
Hear Sarrin singing, brightly, clearly
Hear Rob's voice, "Hello, baby girl"
Hear Claire calling, "Come on, Maddie, get the dog"
Memories keep me company
I am not alone

NONFICTION

Ann Hymes

A QUEEN IN THE GARDEN

A small classified ad in *The Christian Science Monitor* newspaper over forty years ago brought a most interesting visitor into our family:

English woman wishes to be paying guest in American home for one week.

I debated the wisdom of responding to those crisp, intriguing words and then wrote the mystery lady that very day, inviting her to be our non-paying guest in Alexandria, Virginia.

In those days of slower communication and letters making their way across the ocean, it seemed I heard back immediately. Miss Beasley, on her own and recently retired, had never been outside of England. She was looking for a bit of an adventure. We shared correspondence about travel details, and she was excited to accept my invitation and embark on a journey into distant family life. I wasn't surprised to learn that ours was the only response she'd received to her ad. It just seemed natural that we were the home that was waiting for her.

My family has a long history of opening its doors to visitors. As I was growing up, the usual childhood parade of lost and injured animals ended at our house. Baby birds that flew too soon and bunnies huddled in fuzzy clumps without a mother found safety with us. Wild animals in need were simply animals with a different lifestyle. I had a young skunk that I took for walks on a leash as it regained strength and learned its way around the wooded neighborhood. Our own pets always made room for these less domesticated visitors.

My mother's concept of welcome reached beyond sheltering furry and feathered fugitives. Her open-door policy had lessons for living. Once she arranged for a busload of inner-city children from Chicago to spend the day at our suburban home. They played games, music, ran everywhere, danced, and turned the heads of our neighbors. Mother didn't see walls that divide and label. She saw opportunities to broaden thinking.

A Lebanese foreign exchange student came for dinner and stayed a year, teaching our Midwestern family about Middle Eastern food and culture. We children learned that the basis of friendship is the discovery of common ground and the acceptance of differences.

Preparations for Miss Beasley began with a flurry. Our pre-school daughters hauled toys and art projects out of the newly designated guest room. Stray socks and forgotten doll accessories came to light as we pushed around chairs and dressers. A little upheaval reorganizes the familiar. The cat watched all this activity with detached interest, showing no sign of relinquishing her regular spot in the sunny window. For our feline family member, routine ruled without compromise.

The children made welcome signs of paper plates glued to paint-stirring sticks and wrote Miss Beasley's name in big, bright letters. Flowers, happy faces, and pictures of animals representing our home menagerie decorated the signs. I began to wonder if our household would overwhelm the traveler from a solitary, quiet life.

At the airport gate, the crowd kindly gave way to two little girls waving their signs, and Miss Beasley, as unmistakable as a fairy godmother, glowed with a sweet, weary smile at the sight. Her curly white hair was carefully pinned back, with occasional stray tufts that had lost their way. She wore a gray suit and sensible shoes, walking slowly through the parted onlookers. The children excitedly hugged this woman they had never met.

Miss Beasley settled easily into our home. The girls never tired of hearing her read their books with the rolling vowels of her British accent. Familiar characters from *Mr. Egbert Nosh* and *Fox in Socks* took on whole new personalities with the change of voice. She expanded our sense of things.

Miss Beasley surveyed my teapots and chose the small brown pot with yellow stripe instead of the flowery one with gold leaves.

"Very English," she proclaimed.

At tea parties in the garden, my daughters ceremoniously poured orange juice from the little striped pot into multi-colored glasses and put their best manners on display. Even the cat warmed to our visitor, often napping close to the party under the sun-splashed protection of a magnolia tree.

One day the girls made Miss Beasley an elaborate paper crown with large painted jewels and sparkly glitter. We baked chewy chocolate cookies for tea time and piled tiny sandwiches without crusts on silver trays. Sitting outside around a festive table in the garden, with dolls of different heights, stuffed animals, and imaginary guests invited from storybooks, Miss Beasley talked of royal dinners and life in castles and said she felt like the Queen of England on holiday.

She did indeed bring royalty to our home—generosity of spirit and grace, good cheer, and caring. I watched with wonder the easy acceptance of a stranger in our midst, and I remembered the many times my parents had opened our home to what others called "foreigners": immigrants who needed to learn English, refugees, and a Muslim exchange student. Home was for sharing.

Miss Beasley ended up staying two weeks, and her adventure of being part of an American family was also our opportunity for new views about her life and work, which she felt had been uneventful. Our family grew closer by reaching outward, learning that friends are everywhere, waiting to be found. An open door that summer had briefly shortened the distance across the ocean and deepened the language of the heart, providing my children a glimpse of global curiosity.

Toward the end of her visit, Miss Beasley held up her juice glass to the sunlight and asked if she could take it home. We kept in touch for a while, until the letters stopped. I believe she never again left England. The girls and I often thought about Miss Beasley, sipping her juice from a multi-colored glass and remembering her special place in a faraway family. At our last garden party, my five-year-old looked earnestly at Miss Beasley and asked, "Are you the Queen of England?"

Perhaps imagining thrones and robes and people bowing right and left, she asked again, wide-eyed, "Are you really a queen?"

Seated at court with two anxious little faces, surrounded by fragrant blossoms and attentive Teddy bears, Miss Beasley looked at them and replied mischievously, "I do believe I am."

Caroline Kalfas

KNITTING WITH MY GRANDMOTHER

My grandmother owned a green velvet couch that was more ornate than comfy. But there we sat side-by-side.

She was a home economics major with a college degree. I was a girl in elementary school with my legs stretched straight and my brown buckled shoes reaching in the air just beyond the tight cushions. Here, underneath a pastoral oil painting brushed in dark hues, my grandmother taught me to knit, and I am eternally grateful.

With size 8 needles and a yellow skein of cheap polyester yarn, she showed me how to cast on, which I found the most difficult lesson. All of the twisting and looping and learning how to hold the yarn and needles within my awkward digits took time and patience. She worked with her arms around me, holding my hands and guiding my fingers until I could succeed on my own.

"You are a tight knitter," she said, inspecting my work.

This flawed trait made sticking the stiff gray needle into the next circle of fiber difficult. Many times I inadvertently split the yarn and created extra loops. Other times I stabbed too forcefully and accidentally dropped stitches.

Mistakes frustrated me. My grandmother calmed me, taking up the project herself. She peered through her silver-and-blue-metal cat-eye glasses to identify the problem and assured me all was not lost.

While I waited for her to correct my foiled moves, I viewed the decorative fireplace across the room. A delicate green ginger jar and other sparse trinkets adorned the hearth's plain mantle, above which balanced an opulent gold-framed mirror that now hangs in my dining room.

My grandmother's living room has remained vivid in my mind: The tall windows with thick panes of glass. The rough yellow carpet. The white, marble-topped coffee table. A plant stand displaying her collection of blooming pink and purple African violets. Two floral wing-backed chairs. And on the wall, a doorbell of no use to my grandmother, but designed to summon the maid in her historic brick home built for a physician in 1922.

I studied my grandmother's soft, lined face and her short, wavy gray hair that was washed and brushed earlier that morning during her weekly visit to the hair parlor.

My grandmother soon ended the tedious, careful process of recovering lost stitches and lifted the rows of yarn from her lap. Her wrinkled hands suddenly began whizzing, allowing my project to grow a few extra rows before she handed the long needles and scratchy yarn back to me.

I wanted to make a stylish scarf that my grandmother would be proud to wear. I envisioned my grandmother entering her elegant house with the warmth of my hand-knit stole around her neck, or my grandmother inspecting grapefruit at nearby Caroon's supermarket and a friend, by chance shopping at the same time, commenting on her lovely scarf.

"My granddaughter made this for me," she would say with pride, and touch the scarf lightly above her heart. My grandmother would have added a decorative brooch because she liked to wear fancy pins.

But as the scarf progressed, my lack of skills became apparent in the inconsistent size of the rows and occasional holes, some bigger than others. Still, I stitched next to my grandmother, who smelled of Estee Lauder's Youth Dew and Johnson's baby powder. Her short-haired dog, Happy, sat close by on the floor. Through the open window, I could hear the next-door neighbor, Mrs. Poole, practice classical music on her piano. Wind rustled the giant oak trees along the street. The scent of honeysuckles planted along the edge of the cement driveway occasionally wafted through the window screens as we worked.

I took my unfinished project home, relying on my mother to help me progress. Her rows were looser than mine. She added and subtracted stitches to make the rows more even before handing the haphazard strip of yellow back to me.

After many lessons with my mother and grandmother, I was ready to finish the scarf. I thought the accessory must be long enough to wear by now. My grandmother, too, was ready to end the project, but she cautioned me that the strip needed to be longer. I told her I didn't mind a shorter scarf. She showed me how to bind off the stitches, which became my favorite part of knitting because then the project was complete.

I remember the scarf barely reached around my grandmother's neck. Even a broach could not connect the two ends.

"Perhaps this is a doll baby scarf," she suggested.

"Yes!" I agreed with relief and satisfaction. The scarf would fit perfectly around my doll baby. I could make my grandmother another scarf.

But I didn't.

I declared my independence and continued to master the basics of knitting on my own. With practice, I left garter stitches behind and advanced to more intricate patterns. I made buttonholes and sleeves, collars and cuffs. I experimented with various colors, textures, and styles.

During the past 45 years, I have made plenty of sweaters, blankets, and scarves for myself and others, but in all that time, I don't remember ever making my grandmother a scarf or thanking her for teaching me to knit. I should have expressed my gratitude. She passed away more than 10 years ago at the age of 97.

I keep her collection of knitting needles within reach, displayed in an off-white, pineapple-shaped ceramic pitcher near a stash of unused balls of cotton, wool, mohair, and polyester yarn. My gray acrylic and tan bamboo needles blend among her pastel metal ones. Each time I select a pair to begin a new project, I whisper a prayer of thanksgiving and remember my grandmother's gentle patience, skill, voice, and love.

And once in a while when I'm getting dressed for the day, I pin one of her antique brooches to a scarf or sweater I've made and touch the broach lightly over my heart with my own wrinkled hand.

Adrianne Lasker

THE EMBRACE

Tense and frazzled (late again) I tried to rush my un-rushable son to his monthly appointment at Baltimore's Neurology and Autism Center. We hooked arms going up the entry stairs, but PJ suddenly stopped and yanked his arm out of mine.

I had barely noticed the man waiting at the top of the stairs. But my son darted right to him.

Of course, I panicked—he was fast!

Face as black as night, wearing a tattered fatigue jacket, frayed wool cap, leaning heavily on a cane bound in duct tape and capped by a small American Flag. Clinging to the railing in a tight grip, probably contemplating the enormity of descending this avalanche of stairs.

Before I could intervene, PJ, arms outstretched, hugged this old man. The man shied away in fear as my son embraced the stranger with an audible "Awwwwwwww," one of the few sounds PJ is able to make.

The man's downturned mouth seemed to lead the slide of his drooping jowls and wrinkled skin. His yellow eyes looked at my son and me, telling a story of pain, heartbreak, and lost memories.

PJ hugged him long.

The man remained stiff.

Then, perhaps finally remembering the feeling of a loving touch, his head came up. He handed me his cane.

He embraced my son tightly with both arms—and a slight upturn of a smile became unlocked.

When the two separated, the man sharply saluted his new friend, and with a big smile, PJ saluted back.

As we continued on our way, I said "God Bless you."

And the man said, "He just did."

Den Leventhal

THE MAKING OF A MARINER

I had been pretty much a nebbish as a kid. My folks were blue collar. We moved from Philly to Bucks County just before I went into junior high school, where I was given opportunity to learn to play the trombone. But other than music, I had no strong interests. The curiosity that can create a lifelong learner was non-existent up to that point. Then I discovered maps.

My seventh grade geography teacher, Miss Hart, was clearly responsible for what happened. She had speckled grey hair, bound up in a bun, always with a pencil stuck in it. Her default demeanor was a tight-lipped frown. The horn-rimmed glasses accentuated her latent ferocity.

I was fascinated with the atlases, maps, and charts of all kinds that I discovered in her class. She noticed this and put me to work drawing them and reporting on the information that they provided. I learned about political borders, topographical features of the earth, and the socio-economic significance of land masses being divided by rivers, seas, and oceans.

Miss Hart also taught seventh-grade English. The curriculum, if I remember correctly, was half diagramming sentences and half writing book reports. She doled out reading assignments based on the individual student's reading level, but with an attempt to tailor content to individual interests. In my case, she picked titles with travel adventure themes. She started me on Stevenson's *Treasure Island.* This was followed up with Kingsley's *Westward Ho,* a biography of John Paul

Jones, and a story about how Sir Frances Drake defeated the Spanish Armada of 1588 CE.

I was hooked. Seafaring meant travel to foreign places. My recreational reading continued along nautical lines. I started building those plastic ship model kits. Wow. The U.S. Navy had some really cool warships—destroyers, cruisers, battleships—with cannons, torpedoes, and depth charges.

The more I read about ships and seafaring, the more I wanted the real thing. I wanted to know what it felt like to actually move across water in a boat. Before my seventh-grade year was finished, I learned that there was something called Sea Scouts, and there was a troop in the nearby town of Bristol, located on the banks of the Delaware River.

Pestering my mom worked fine. (My dad didn't want anything to do with water for reasons I never learned). So I got a sailor suit and was attending monthly meetings at a local parish house where the pastor, Reverend O'Conner, served as troop leader. I learned knot tying, chart reading, anchoring, boat terminology, and other delightful maritime lore.

The best part was having a boat on which we applied our seafaring skills during summer months. It was a 32-foot-long, double-ender, carvel-built wooden whaleboat. There were eight oars, four to a side. It also had a 30-horsepower inboard engine with a single screw. Steering was by tiller.

Putting on my seaman's garb prior to a meeting made me quiver in anticipation. During the summer months, we'd meet at the parish house two, sometimes three, times a month. We then piled into the good reverend's truck for transport to a marina on Neshaminy Creek, south of Bristol, where our boat was docked. We'd motor out of the creek onto the river and puddle about, learning to keep a lookout, ship oars and row, anchor, tie up to the public pier at Bristol, and keep out of the way of the giant ore boats that steamed up river to the steel plant near Trenton.

One nifty lesson involved our troop leader deliberately jamming the boat onto a mud bank. Our job was to figure out how to get it back into deeper water without getting mud sucked up into the motor's water intake system. We succeeded—returning to port wet, muddy, and gleeful.

And then, one of the scouts, Tony, came to a few of us with an idea. He lived in Tullytown, a predominately Italian-American community just north of Bristol. Tony was a natural-born organizer. He was tall, thin, with dark hair, and dark eyes that squinted at the world as if looking for an opportunity to take advantage of anything.

"Guys, how'd ya like to earn a few bucks?"

We looked at each other. Tony was full of ideas—mostly crazy and unworkable.

"Look, this is legit. My uncle owns some bars and he needs help with transporting stuff he uses in the bars."

Fat Johnny said, "We're just kids. What can we do? Ya mean moving boxes in a storeroom? Or what?"

"Nah, this is big time stuff," said Tony with a grin.

"Okay, so spit it out. What's your idea?" Billy was skeptical. He'd previously gotten expelled from school for three days because he followed Tony into one of his numerous escapades.

"My uncle wants us to transport a bunch of boxes across the river."

I said, "That doesn't make any sense. Your uncle can send one of his trucks across the river to pick up stuff."

Tony's grin got even wider. "He can't use his trucks. Ya see, it's against the law for people in Pennsylvania to buy liquor in Jersey and bring the bottles back here."

"Why?"

"It's a matter of tax. The government here taxes booze and Jersey doesn't. So it's cheaper in Jersey. If someone brings a case of booze across the bridge from Jersey and the state cops catch him, they can take his truck and put him in the hoosegow. But if my uncle can get the bottles for his bars from across the river, he can save a lot of money, and if we can do the transport, he'll pay us for each load."

Billy grimaced. "How can we do that?"

"By boat of course." Tony beamed in appreciation of his own genius.

I smiled back. *Smuggling.* Having just finished reading Orczy's *The Scarlet Pimpernel*, my mind was filled with images of smuggling across the English Channel during the French Revolution.

Then I had another thought. "You're crazy if you think we can use our Sea Scout boat for smuggling."

Tony sighed. "Where do we stay when we do a two-day training out on the water?"

"Billy's house of course. He lives right next to the marina. But how do we get O'Conner to let us use the boat?"

Tony's grin returned. "We don't need to. I pressed the engine key into a bar of soap and got a cousin who works in a machine shop to make a copy. When O'Conner goes home Saturday night, we'll make a run up to Trenton and get back before morning."

I looked at him in silence. This was wild.

Tony said, "You've got the river chart and can navigate. Billy can get gas from his dad's shed and can run the engine. Johnny will crew and I'm the business manager."

How could I resist? A smuggler on the river? How cool is that? I said, "I'm in."

Billy asked, "How much do we get?"

"Twenty-five bucks each for one trip."

That seemed to nail it. Over the next two years, we managed to pull off three trips each summer. The excitement of each trip was amazing. Shortly after dark, we'd go into the marina, gas up, cast off, and motor slowly out of Neshaminy Creek.

The passage up the Delaware River was easy. I was thrilled to be the navigator, in charge of piloting our craft to its goal. The channel was well marked with lateral buoys, and we steered from one buoy to another by magnetic compass, using the chart to determine the course directions.

In summer, the air over the river was cool and permeated with variegated aromas from the passing shoreline. The smells ranged from petroleum to pine. There was no river traffic at night, so it was a safe passage.

Arriving at a condemned pier on the south end of Trenton, the capital of New Jersey, three flashes of a flashlight would elicit a corresponding reply from a vehicle waiting on shore. Billy would nudge our boat dockside, and then Johnny and I would jump onto the pier to secure bow and stern lines. The guys on the truck would bring cases of booze out onto the pier and we would stack them into our vessel. My main job was to ensure we didn't overload or create a list. Tony tallied the cases as required by his uncle.

On the return trip, we would dock at the public pier in Bristol, where the same truck would be waiting for us. After discharging our cargo, we returned to the marina, tied up, and snuck back into Billy's house. The next day we awaited the good Reverend dockside for our outing on the river, feeling smug with the knowledge of our shared adventure.

Our smuggling career lasted two summers. The Reverend O'Conner's suspicions were aroused one day after Billy forgot to refill the gas tank. Our scout leader checked the engine's running hours meter against his log book and realized that he hadn't noticed the gaps in the ending and starting times, indicating unaccounted-for running times in the log.

He told us he suspected someone in the marina was using our boat and had reported his suspicions to the local constabulary. At that point, we knew our career as smugglers was over.

I don't know what happened later in life to the others in our smuggling crew. For my part, a family friend learned of my interest in seafaring. He introduced me to the United States Merchant Marine Academy (Kings Point), one of our five federal military service academies. A graduate, class of 1944, and captain of a large tanker, he connected my passion with a road map into my future.

His introduction to this school was electrifying. From that point on, I had only one goal in life, to become a Kings Point cadet. That goal turned out to be critical to my personal and professional development in life. The academy instilled a sense of duty and responsibility that became the ground of all my endeavors following graduation in 1962, after which I traversed oceans, rivers, and continents. But my early exposure to literary adventuring ensured I never lost that lacing of romantic anticipation as I explored our world.

I often think back to Miss Hart. She kickstarted my entry to the maritime world. It's a shame that great teachers often never learn of what they created with the human materials they mold.

Barbara Lockhart

TWENTY-TWO ACRES, MORE OR LESS

Dreams ... A black sedan, looking every bit like a tin lizzie, pulled up alongside the barn, and Mrs. Waldon, accompanied by others I probably once knew, was fanning herself with her glove. Her face was flushed, and she repeated over and over, "Drive me to Florida, will you? My blood pressure's up."

The pea vines in bloom stretched out in long green fields to the horizon, their fragrance surrounding us in sweetness. It was a place one might be drawn to, although rarely come upon, in the natural course of things. A table appeared at the close end of the rows as the women climbed out of the car. I remembered only then, a call I had had at some time about someone asking to come visit the farm. I must have said yes. I remembered the question only vaguely and understood nothing about the reason, but had a feeling that things I had neglected were catching up with me and that I had, after all, this wonderful land surrounded by serenity. Why not share it? Four women began holding fans of cards, then there were six of them, then eight, seated at a table that kept stretching toward the horizon, a table that was suddenly set with clear drinks and clinking ice cubes. I remember thinking, "They're no trouble—even brought their own drinks." They paid no attention to me, but Mrs. Waldon repeated, "Can we go now to Florida?" and I let someone else take her after being nebulous about any commitment, thinking she should see a doctor first.

Someone commented on a hill that stood next to the barn, and I explained it was all our trouble; it was where we saved all the bad things that had happened to us, and we covered them with soil to keep them contained. It was the burial of bad times. They nodded. They understood and kept on playing cards, while I was mindful of the vastness of the fields in the hazy, pink light of a setting sun, the silence as the afternoon waned, and of how alone we all are and how minuscule in the great space.

One of the women, who wore her hair in a bun, turned to a petite slip of a woman with short, straight, white hair, who was dressed in a cotton housedress and a blue cardigan, and said to her with impatience, "Oh, just discard, Mary. We can't wait all afternoon."

The dream came again and again. The women haunted me as I battled with my new station in life, that of a single woman in a wilderness of hundreds of acres of woods bordered by cornfields that stretched all the way to the state road, a mile and a half away. The lights from town, seven miles away, offered a bit of comfort, but actually very little. Within one year, our family of five had dissipated, off to the city and other worlds. At the farm, it was just me and the cat. My worries and strained forbearance occurred in my dreams. I was too busy earning a living when awake. The one constant in my life was my job teaching at a local, rural school in a nearby town. A joy, it was, actually. A distraction from my new single life.

Reality hit hardest at night, where I was introduced to that status in life you never think will happen to you. I was aware of the fact that in town the women gathered, Evelyn, Bootsie, Virginia, Mary Lou, Miss Suzie, and Juanita and nameless others, on Tuesdays and Thursdays to play bridge, outdoing each other with delicious dishes heavy with mayonnaise and cream served with the latest news from the gossip bench. They dressed carefully for such occasions. And in the country, another widow busied herself with pruning her 100 rose bushes to glorious bloom. Down the road, another widow closed her blinds and was never seen except to arrive at church on Sunday morning. Another who lived at the edge of a field, raised a vegetable garden, fed and killed her chickens, and kept track of who was playing bridge that afternoon and where. I had a feeling my story wasn't new or modern or in any way different from the women around me or before me, that there was a long history of women left or widowed who had made their way for generations in this rural land.

In town, there is plenty of evidence of times past: where the stagecoach came through, the exact spot where slave auctions were held, which historic house had a ballroom, where the wealthy landowners and professionals lived, where tanners and blacksmiths had their shops along streets hardened with oyster shells. It is a history well preserved in the placards along the road with dates and names for tourists who might be fascinated by such scant detail. The women are never mentioned. But look further; the land is rich with history. It takes some digging, though, and maybe first-hand experience in what life in these parts was like, and is like now, especially for women alone. Theirs is largely a silent history, untold and uneventful. Its name is *Coping*. Has anyone honored those who monitored and managed the fields that surrounded them? Keeping the old homestead vital? Staying?

Among the list of landowners of my twenty-two acres are three women: Elizabeth Burton, Nettie Adshead, and me. I wondered about Elizabeth in particular, because of her status as a free black woman in pre-Civil War times, when a woman alone was tempting for those who would take the land from her. How she made her way alone and raised four children, in a time of untold tension and oppression, set me off to imaging her life and researching the times. Her story appears again and again in my writing as it is one of immense courage and strength, or so I imagined. But then again, she had no choice but to struggle to survive. She lost the farm in 1857, when it was returned to white ownership. Shadrack Murphy, a poor, illiterate farmer, got it cheap at auction upon her death. Years later, the farm was a wedding gift to his daughter, Nettie Adshead. It was she and her husband, George, who built the present house in 1909, making the house 110 years old this year.

Here Nettie raised five children, and it wasn't until 1949 that indoor plumbing, electricity, and a bathroom were installed. There was a tiled porch kitchen, a living room with sliding doors, a dining room, an arched room off to the sunny side of the house, and three bedrooms. By 1966, kerosene stoves had been set in the fireplaces. When we moved in, I noted old varieties of roses in the garden, along with lilacs and hollyhocks, as well as a huge bush of sage. I wondered how Nettie supported herself after the children left and her husband died. A family member told me she raised chickens and drove to the nearest town every Saturday, donning a hat and white gloves along with her next-to-best dress, to sell eggs. There was also the rent she collected for the land tilled by her neighbor. She was in her eighties when she died in 1966. The house stood empty from then until 1971 when our family moved in. We bought it despite the broken windows, the ivy growing profusely in one of the bedrooms, and a beehive that clung to the wall where honey had dripped down in hardened brown rivulets. The walls were covered with peeling wallpaper that wavered in the breeze. Uncovering the walls, we found oyster shells mixed with horse hair and plaster, causing a shower of loosened and dried wall whenever a door was slammed. However, nothing deterred us in the old days. We had vision and promise and wild hope in our youth. I never once really considered Nettie Adshead and her solitary existence on these twenty-two acres, her tenacity to remain in a place that kept her separate and alone—until I was in the same circumstance.

My connection with the land didn't begin immediately. We were too concerned with restoring the house and adjusting to a seven-mile drive to pick up a loaf of bread or container of milk. And my children, coming from the city, were adjusting to a rural school that was newly integrated, where unrest, fighting, and prejudice were at their worst. Our land was farmed by a neighbor farmer who'd rented the land from us, and because it was farmed as it had been for 150 years, we didn't walk on it. It was just there, growing corn or soybeans, irrigated at intervals in the long hot summers. We watched migrant workers come in to pick tomatoes and watermelon, and were astonished when they approached the house, barefoot and weary, to ask for a drink of water from our hose. It was a world we had had no preparation for, an eye-opening education in how another world worked. In love with the old trees surrounding the house, my husband assured me it would all work out. And it did, for a while. We had horses, chickens, rabbits, pigs, ducks, dogs, cats, and collections of turtles and snakes. In winter we skated on the pond that covered an acre. We had a huge garden that produced a mountain of string beans that much to my initial dismay, covered the entire kitchen table as the beans waited to be washed, cut and frozen, a task that took days. We learned to slaughter the pigs and butcher the meat, a task that found me in the house covering my ears to dispel the sound of a gunshot to a Barney's head and the lowering of his body into a trough to scrape the bristles off his hide.

Meanwhile, the old house was rejuvenated and made livable. We were going back in time to a green space that promised self-sufficiency. We even had a solar system that heated our water.

However, somewhere along the line, I began to identify with Miss Nettie, who had lived on the farm and left jars of blackberry jam dated 1952 in the cellar. We'd found her rocking chair in the chicken coop when we first bought the house. There was the old pump organ in the tack shed, and a Hoosier cabinet in the barn, and a lady's button boot somewhere in the surrounding woods along with old jars and pots. What traces of our time on this old farm would we leave? That Miss Nettie was alone was now my fate, as the children and husband found a different path and I was left with what I became painfully aware of—the incessant wind screaming through windows and cracks, storms that tore down branches from the old trees and caused some of them to crash to the ground with a shocking tearing sound and terrifying crack, the silence of the old house broken only by the refrigerator and the roar of the furnace on winter afternoons, the dried-up well, the bright moonlit landscape that crept through the windows and disallowed sleep, the encroaching brush that I was powerless to tame—and the solitude. I hadn't noticed these things when teenagers filled the rooms and the husband was ready for dinner and filling the woodstove with logs, back when the house was filled with the sounds of an electric guitar until four in the morning.

I thought a lot about Elizabeth, too, whose story had occurred 150 years before. She'd been vulnerable to losing the land from the start. And she did lose it, five years after buying it. Single women in the past have been easy prey. I suppose I was easy prey, too. A threat of losing half my land occurred when my neighbor sued me, claiming half my field was his despite my having the deed and tax bills to prove it. After three court proceedings, including the appellate court in Annapolis, I won. This is only worth mentioning because it changed the course of my life on the farm, my appreciation of the land, and my determination to preserve that twenty-two-acre patch of land for many reasons: the history of its dimensions since 1843, the constant spraying of chemicals on the fields close to the house, the expanse of land I wanted to enjoy, the chance to watch a forest grow, the chance for wildlife to enter and stay, the regard for the natural order of things, and the chance to simply walk in the woods. Maybe I needed a new beginning. A revival. Fighting to keep the land changed me. It gave me purpose—an unexpected, unplanned one, one that might hold an extension of the meaning of my life at this point, or maybe an actualization of who I am and what I believe.

So we planted trees on twenty acres of bare field. I say *we*. After a few years, after having tried the cities and running into a few obstacles, my kids, one by one, returned to the shore. They, and their kids, now walked out across the field with me with shovels in hand and buckets full of white pine and loblolly seedlings about a foot high. In the cold spring air, with the wind slamming across the emptiness, I dreamed of a forest, yet looked doubtfully at the seedlings, thousands of them purchased for pennies from the state tree farm nursery. It seemed so hopeless a task, such a foolish undertaking that would take decades to come to fruition, and digging in the hard earth with the children growing tired and complaining—the only thing growing was the doubt in my heart. We planted for days that stretched into weeks.

The neighboring farmers were dismayed. "Ya know how long it takes to clear a field? What, are ya crazy? You're cancelling your rent money, as well as the government subsidies for the farmer who rents it. Ya messin' up the path of the irrigation system. Geez! Fair enough for a 'come-here'."

Yeah. Well. Anyway. We walked the boundaries, a good distance from the house, which stood in one corner of the plot of twenty-two acres. Ownership was not on my mind. The land would only be borrowed for a little while, when it would be passed on. The land stretched before me, frighteningly even, and I began to wonder if I *was* crazy. It was a lot to handle, yet in the end, I realized I didn't have to handle anything. I just had to observe, and enjoy its return to the wild. There was something very satisfying about that. But then, I wasn't a farmer.

When weeds began to take over the field, my son, Jacob, with his usual calming foresight, brought over his tractor and made paths throughout the field, paths that crisscrossed and folded back on themselves, that made clear the boundaries, paths that wound around the pond and led to the house, again and again, and meandered far from the house to the neighboring farm and back. In addition to the pines, I planted dogwood and redbud along some of the paths, and later added sawtooth oaks, white oaks, and chestnut trees. Some trees just appeared—a grove of river birch and a single peach tree, along with wild rose vines and blackberry bushes, milkweed, and hundreds of American holly. While the trees were still young and the paths still sunny, the wild flowers that appeared thrilled me: wild clematis, asters, and sunflower varieties, Queen Anne's lace, clover, and in the deepening shade, ferns. Honeysuckle draped among the trees growing in great long ropes, bringing spring.

I only had to mow the paths. It never seemed like an awesome task. I was quite happy to mow. But mainly, I was happiest at walking the paths, watching and naming things that appeared. It brought me faith in the earth to revive, to cleanse itself of chemicals with the rain, to reseed and propagate, and bring pleasure. I worry that some of what we've done on this earth will not allow revival, but faith that it will come back remains, although that might be without us. In just twenty years, the trees are tall, and the paths are covered with pine needles. New species appear now and then, discoveries to be made every time I walk. A quiet peaceful place, so alive, just going about its business. My church, I think.

The crowd of wildlife makes its presence known, but discreetly and orderly. Eagles and hawks abound, songbirds, fox, possums, ground hogs, and turkeys. The worn down deer paths tell us the deer are there, although we rarely see them. During drought, they come down to the pond for a drink, so we know they're around. Occasionally, a heron stalks at the edge of the pond, and ducks and geese test the waters.

Somehow, I've grown along with the forest. With that comes a reunion with the good times this place, which we still call the farm, has afforded me. Somewhere, traveling out in the universe, difficult times float away, and it takes real effort to bring them to the fore. It's the pleasures we remember mostly, like a gift. They seem to come in closer as one grows older. If life can come back to a bare, chemically infused field so prolifically, then there must be a plan written somewhere that a genesis is available in other places, too—a wise word to those of us who linger in a place of perpetual dichotomy, somewhere between hope and hopelessness.

A number of seasons ago, a cold spell of single digits descended for a few days. With the furnace running almost constantly, and the ground frozen hard after a wet fall where the trees now stood in shallow puddles throughout the woods, a walk meant the danger of a twisted ankle as crunching underfoot, the ice lay along the paths and skimmed the pond. For a few days, I didn't venture out. Then a phone call around 6 p.m. on a Sunday evening.

"Mom? Meet us down at the pond? We're going skating."

Another unexpected gift. The moments for which I live are just this: the offer of a bit of fun coming out of the dark, the excitement because of the dark, the daring to skate down in the woods on a clear, still night, when one cannot even see the edges of the pond or a blade of grass encased in ice that might catch a skate, the twig lying on the surface ready to send anyone sprawling. The embrace of danger. More than that though, there was my son's planning. He'd inspected the ice, gathered twigs for a fire in the afternoon and piled them high in the center of the pond, right on the ice, and then brought me a chair so I could sit safely with the fire at my feet, none of which I knew when I saw the flashlight in my driveway and heard the two of them, Jacob, and my granddaughter, Sara, coming toward me. Jacob was full of assurances that the ice was firm enough, and besides he had his cell phone if we needed it and the folding chair for me while Sara dragged a sled for "the both of us."

After the fire caught, he sat on the sled to put on his skates, the creases around his eyes sharply defined by the light of the fire, reminding me that despite the persistence of time we are fortunate to keep certain parts of us alive through all the changes. Sara, giggling, tried to push me as I sat in the chair; then gave up. Without skates herself, I offered my size 8's, but she only wears a 5. "It's okay," she said. "Dad will take me for a ride on the sled."

Soon Jacob was skating around us as we hovered by the fire. "You see how the wind is coming out of the southwest," he said. "Unusual."

The smoke shifted even though the air was still, as if there were spirits awakened by the sounds of us, my granddaughter chatting about new skates maybe her mother would buy for her the next day, and the *crisp, crisp* sound of Jacob's skates. He was speeding now, with an abandonment not visible in recent years. Prodigal, like a homecoming we rarely experience as we get older, but instantly recognizable and reassuring, he skated magnificently despite all the years away from the ice.

"Come on, Mom. Get on the sled. I'll pull you and Sara."

My trust was complete as I got on the sled, Sara between my legs, my arms around her. We were off, and Jacob spun us into a whiplash, the sled skimming sideways across the ice. I screamed and laughed, sounds that astonished me because I hadn't screamed or laughed liked that for a hundred years and all it took was a hair-raising slide across the ice. I was aware of my son's strength as he held onto the rope of the sled so that we didn't fly off into the trees at the edge of the pond. Pausing for a breath, I heard the ice crack, a loud muffled thud.

"Don't worry, Mom. It's only the stress cracks at the edge of the pond."

I believed him. I believe in him. I believe in fun, in screaming in the dark with the light from the house streaming across the ice, the tall shadows of the mature trees reaching us, the crackling of the fire and the melted ice at its base, the wonder of heat rising so that there could be such a thing as a fire built on the ice. Most of all I believe in the generations we are, in the generations of the land itself, in replenishment on even the coldest night, the bold human spirit that sparks unexpectedly, the details of callused hands building a fire in the dark, the old skate hook saved all those years with which to tighten laces, a granddaughter's mittened hand orchestrating the hope of new skates.

In time, they helped me off the ice, Jacob on one side, Sara on the other. Feeling my helplessness at stepping to the edge of the pond, my only comment, laughingly, was, "If this is the way it's going to be in a few years, I don't want to play!" But when something fills you to the brim, it seems like even death will be all right, saying good-bye possible after being so well fulfilled.

Just before we stepped to the bank, Jacob held the flashlight downward and through the clear ice were bright green shoots, waiting among last year's debris from the trees. He said he saw tadpoles swimming under the ice earlier in the afternoon. We walked toward the house, toward the light that is to be kept lit for occasions such as this, giving reason for everything I've known here on these twenty-two acres.

A slight thaw the next day. Even with the warming temperatures, there was a promise of snow. I walked around the pond, the remains of the fire sunk below the surface with the melted ice, a few scars on the skin of ice still showing the path of Jacob's blades. The day turned grey as the clouds gathered, but I carried the memory of the night before, which still warmed me even in the bitter wind. It had all turned out okay.

The renewal of family, the emerging and maturing forest, the privilege of living so close to nature, the old house with lighted windows in the midst of the darkness, reminded me that if you waited long enough, things usually turned out okay. The tall trees from twelve-inch seedlings said so.

Russell Reece

THE COTTAGE AT SLAUGHTER BEACH

Sometimes dreams come true, even when they shouldn't. That thought crossed my mind the cold and gloomy Saturday in December 1996 when I pulled into the driveway of my partially renovated cottage at Slaughter Beach. It had been several months and many awkward sessions with a marriage counselor since I had last seen the place. I hoped a visit would lift my spirits.

The new concrete piers, vinyl siding, and replacement windows gleamed, but the entrance steps and deck already looked weathered from the salt air. Still, it was a far cry from the condition of the cottage when we'd bought it eighteen months before.

I got out of the car and pulled up my collar against icy gusts coming off the bay. The adjacent houses were closed up tight for the season. A storm window on my neighbor's second-story bedroom hung askew and banged in the wind. I climbed the front steps, turned the key and pushed open the door. The rubber weather stripping that had held firm for months separated with a sharp ripping sound.

Owning a cottage at Slaughter Beach had been a dream of ours since that weekend in 1969 when Dianne and I spent a Friday night with Bill and Charlotte Jarrell in their rental on Bay Avenue. Bill was the singer with the Banjo Dusters and had a three-day gig at a tavern in Rehoboth. He decided to make a vacation out of it and had taken a cottage for the week. We were friends with the Jarrells and followed the band wherever they played. It wasn't the kind of music most couples in their early twenties went in for, but we liked the nights out and the fun that always happened whenever the Banjo Dusters performed.

Bill had given us directions from Argo's Corner. As we drove in, the peaceful countryside and lush Sussex County farmland was a welcome change from the frantic city landscapes back home. Early on we had turned off the radio so we could enjoy it all without distraction. But then we passed a stretch of tangled woods and the terrain turned to a broad expanse of marsh and tidal mudflats. A flooded ditch ran along both sides of the road. Off in the hazy distance stood a row of what looked like ramshackle buildings, and we began to wonder just what kind of place Slaughter Beach was.

We made the turn onto Bay Avenue and it was as if we had stepped back in time. The old one- and two-story clapboard cottages sat side-by-side on narrow waterfront lots. As we searched for the address, we were charmed by the mix of gingerbread and simple beach-influenced architecture, the picket fences, the gardens, driftwood sculptures, the unusual outbuildings.

A few kids rode past on bikes, but for a beachfront community in the middle of summer it seemed surprisingly devoid of people. We pulled into the side-yard of Bill's rental and he came off the screened porch and welcomed us. The weather had been unbearably hot and humid, but at the cottage, the soft, off-water breeze cut the humidity. It was noticeably quiet, the only sounds birdsong and the gentle rattling of cord-grass and reeds in the adjacent lot. Standing next to the car, it felt as if the pace of things had just slowed down a little.

Bill's cottage was across the road from the beach and backed up to a small wood-line that fronted the marsh, which now seemed more interesting and inviting than it had on our drive in. We got settled then walked across the road to look at the water. Beyond the wide, grass-covered dune was a sandy beach littered here and there with driftwood, shells, and a few horseshoe crabs. Looking north, the shoreline made a gradual curve that extended out to the old Mispillion Lighthouse. Several small boats—Hobie-cats, Sunfish, and aluminum johnboats—were pulled up against the dune, many marked with the address of the owner's cottage. There couldn't have been more than ten or twelve people on the entire beach, which we found astounding.

That night we were at the tavern through last call and helped the band break down and load up before making the easy drive back to the cottage. It was a clear night and we weren't ready to turn in, so we walked over and sat on the beach for a while. Several ships were at the anchorage, their lights twinkling in the distance. Stars were bright and the breeze off the bay was fresh and cool. Behind us, the beachfront cottages sat silhouetted against the moonlit sky.

In the morning we hung out on the porch and drank coffee. Bill, in a bathing suit and flip-flops, walked down the block to the store for a carton of milk. He was gone for ten minutes and not one car went down the main drag. It was then that Dianne said out loud what we had both been thinking. "It would be nice to have a place down here. It's so comfortable and close to everything." That was the start of the dream.

But it wasn't one we could act upon at the time. Dianne was working as a teller at a local bank while I worked a part-time job and went to school on the GI bill. We were barely making ends meet and had very little left over after paying the mortgage and the minimum balances on our credit cards. I would graduate in two years, but we had been waiting to start a family so it wasn't likely we would have money for a summer place for quite a while. But the seed had been planted.

For several years after that, on our weekend trips to Rehoboth, we often cruised through Slaughter Beach. We stopped on the road and looked at cottages that were for sale, frequently calling agents and asking prices, knowing any price would be too much. Somehow the act of calling made it seem as if we were getting closer to having our own place. I graduated and started a new job. We had our first child, a daughter. And then in 1973 a bay-front lot went up for sale: 50 feet of frontage for $2000. It was an ordinary piece of land, 250 feet long and covered end-to-end with a 10-foot-tall stand of phragmites. It was perfect. We had almost a thousand in savings and borrowed the rest from my brother-in-law. We were in.

For the next four summers, we took frequent daytrips to the lot. Our son was born. We lugged the port-a-crib, hibachi, and umbrella out onto the beach and spent days picnicking and beach-combing, imagining our cottage sitting on the lot behind us, imagining long summers here as the kids grew up and Dianne and I grew old together relaxing on our deck overlooking the bay. We collected house plans and ideas from decorating magazines, picked up pamphlets from builders, got quotes on septic systems and the installation of electrical service, anything we could do without spending money kept the dream alive and gave the illusion we were moving forward.

But then things got all jumbled up. The kids were growing and we needed some money. Almost magically we received a letter from a real-estate agent offering to purchase the Slaughter Beach property for many times more than we had paid for it. I had a new job that was very demanding, leaving little time for spending days at the beach with the family, so we sold the lot. If things worked out the way we hoped, we could go back in a few years and buy any cottage we wanted.

But the years went by, the kids grew up and went their own ways, the career blossomed. We were always busy. There wasn't time for dreams anymore, or the lazy weekends we had enjoyed so much back in the early seventies. We did very well for ourselves, but in the midst of our success, something had changed with the marriage.

In the spring of 1995 we learned that a fixer-upper cottage in the old section of Slaughter Beach was on the market. "The bay-front property alone was worth the price," the agent said. We drove out to see it. The place was a wreck. Not one other cottage on the beach was in a worse state of repair. It would need to be jacked up, pilings installed, new siding and windows, completely gutted and re-done on the inside. We wondered if it was even salvageable. Someone would have to be crazy to take on a project like this. But as we wandered out on the dune and looked at the derelict building, possibilities of all kinds seemed to assert themselves. I looked at the cottage next door with its friendly grouping of deck chairs, and out on the beach where a couple with two small children relaxed at the edge of the water. The old dreams began to stir again.

Two years later, on that cold December afternoon, I stepped into the kitchen over piles of shattered plaster and construction debris. The old porcelain sink and ripped linoleum countertop were thick with dust and littered with Styrofoam cups and crumpled McDonald's wrappers. In the big room, the furniture that had come with the house had been pushed to the side and stacked haphazardly. Unfinished wires dangled from the locations of new light fixtures and receptacles. Ragged wall edges and exposed two-by-fours surrounded the newly framed replacement windows.

Six months after we bought the place, the problems with our marriage had become overwhelming. We had the contractors finish the outside of the building and then stopped the renovation. The cottage sat idle as we went through months of counseling, where we tried to revisit and rekindle elements of our relationship that had been good and meaningful, things that had brought us together in the first place.

I stared out the back window at the dune and the bay beyond. I thought of Bill and Charlotte Jarrell and the fun we used to have following the Banjo Dusters. I thought of that moonlit night in 1969 when Slaughter Beach had first come alive for us and the joy we felt imagining our cottage, our years of happy dreams. But everything seemed muted now, lost amidst anger and uncertainty.

A sheet of old gray wallpaper, its original flowered pattern barely discernable, drooped on the wall by the backdoor. I tried to imagine this wallpaper when it was new, how it would have freshened and brightened this dingy space. I tried. It just wasn't in me anymore.

Jeff Scott

WHY REAL MEN CRY AT BOSTON SYMPHONY HALL

"Wednesday, May 26, 1999, was the best day of my life!" I exclaimed.

"Thanks a LOT, DAD!" came the reply from my 10-year-old daughter in the back seat of the car as she feigned displeasure. "I thought the day I was born was the best day of your life! Or maybe the day Josh was born? Or the day you got married?"

"Listen, kid," I bantered back, "don't ask the question if you can't handle the answer."

My wife gave me a knowing look and smiled. We both consider our wedding day to be a pretty cool day, but the day provided so much stress that neither of us would say it was the best day of our life.

Nope. For me, the best day of my life thus far in my 43 years was Wednesday, May 26, 1999. I was 23 years old. For my birthday (or maybe it was Christmas; I don't remember) my wife had purchased tickets to see John Williams conduct the Boston Pops Orchestra at the world-famous Boston Symphony Hall. John Williams was sort of a hero of mine. Why? Because John Williams made *Star Wars*. No, he did not direct or produce *Star Wars*, but he wrote the score. The music. The music which I'd argue helped make *Star Wars* into the epic it is.

It certainly wasn't the acting—with all due respect to Mark Hamill, Harrison Ford, and Carrie Fisher (may her beautiful, tender heart rest in peace, sigh ...)—and it wasn't even the special effects. There are a lot of awesome things about the movie production of the original three

Star Wars films, but nothing is as great as the music. I can hear the theme now and so can you, even if you've never seen it. Granted, the idea that someone hasn't seen at least the original *Star Wars* released in 1977 is baffling to me, but I know those people exist. I'm married to one. But I am relatively confident that if a person hears any of the many pieces from the score of *Star Wars*, they'd recognize it even if they'd never seen the movie. t's that well known.

There is no way to overstate the influence Williams has had on Hollywood. He wrote the scores for all of the Indiana Jones movies, *Jaws*, the Harry Potter films, *Close Encounters of the Third Kind*, the original *Superman* movie, *Saving Private Ryan*, *E. T.*, *J.F.K.*, *Hook*, *Lincoln*, *A.I.*, *Home Alone*, *Seven Years in Tibet*, the most recent *War of the Worlds*, *The BFG*. The list just goes on and on and on. The man is a musical genius. For the purposes of brevity, I'll not continue to discuss his accolades. That's why *Wikipedia* exists.

I was first introduced to Williams by my maternal grandmother. It wasn't a personal introduction, just the introduction of the idea that classical music can be cool. My grandmother was a classical music lover. She began playing the violin when she was young, majored in music in college, and stuck with it until she died in her eighties. I used to tell people she played with the Boston Pops. This isn't true, but she was a good violinist in my eyes and the Boston Pops were good in everyone's eyes, so it didn't seem all that far-fetched. Also, she's dead now and we'll let legends be legendary. At any rate, I remember sheepishly telling Grandma I didn't really like classical music. I thought it was boring and it put me to sleep.

"I bet you do like it, you just don't know it," she said.

"Nah, not really."

"Do you know who John Williams is?" she asked. "He is the conductor of the Boston Pops."

I answered with a blank stare.

"He composed the music for Star Wars."

This piqued my interest. "Really?"

"Yes. And Indiana Jones, and E.T.!"

"Really?"

"Yes, really."

I didn't jump onto the classical music train immediately, but I was fascinated by the idea of music and movies. I guess I had just taken music in movies for granted, like it was just something that was part of the movie. And it is. But it is such an important part of the movie experience. The music brings out the emotion in the movie. Take *Jaws*, for instance. Before you see any shark, you hear that music, Da-DUM, and you know the shark is coming. And you're scared for the lady who has made the decision to swim in the ocean all alone at a crazy hour. She's toast and everybody but her knows it! But without the emotion of the moment, brought about by the music John Williams wrote, you might not care as much. He is so good at what he does. And I've loved his music ever since that conversation with Grandma. I loved it before that conversation; I just didn't know it.

For the next decade or so, as I began to recognize and appreciate movie scores, seeing John Williams in person was a goal of mine. I wanted to see an orchestra directed by him playing movie music composed by him. And given my lifelong residence in the Boston area, I would prefer this orchestra to be the Boston Pops. My wife knew this and she bought me tickets to see him on Wednesday, May 26, 1999. He would be conducting the Boston Pops and they would be playing some pieces from his movies.

My memories from that day are vivid. I was so excited! I remember getting ready for the date in our apartment. I remember how it was a perfect evening in May, my favorite month. I remember the black Dodge Stratus we were driving. I remember listening to the radio on the way. The DJ came on and said something about a special event at Boston Symphony Hall. Since I was driving to an event at that very place I turned up the volume:

The Boston Pops will be performing the world premiere of the music from Star Wars: Phantom Menace *tonight ....*

Trying to control my emotions, I looked at Joy and asked if she knew we were going to the world premiere of the score from the latest and much anticipated Star Wars movie. She did not, but I could see in her eyes she was happy, too. She was happy not so much about the music, but happy because I was happy. Know what I mean?

When we arrived at the concert hall, we received our programs and sat down to await the start of the performance. I looked through the program. It was the kind of program that isn't made just for the night you are there but for a whole season. So it had the schedule and line-up for every Boston Pops performance for the 1999 season. This included the pieces the orchestra would play, the name of the conductors, and the name of special guest solo artists if there were any. If I remember correctly, Williams was conducting three performances that week and we were in attendance for the last one. As I looked through the program I noted the night before Itzhak Perlman had performed. This was the one disappointing moment for me. Itzhak Perlman is a virtuoso violinist. He is to the violin what Yo Yo Ma is to the cello, Robin Williams was to comedy, Ted Williams was to hitting a baseball, Walt Disney was to animation. He's the best. I turned to my wife and said, "Shoot! We missed Itzhak Perlman. That is the only thing that could have made this night any better. Maybe he'll just show up tonight too because he's Itzhak Perlman and he can do what he wants." I grinned at her, knowing I was asking a bit much.

My grandmother had also told me about Itzhak Perlman. I think when I was small I had even gone to see him with my mother and grandmother. It's one of those things that is actually a pretty big deal, but as a kid you had no idea. I remember them being so excited about a concert we were going to. I also remember falling asleep during the concert. This was before the John Williams conversation with grandma, and my dozing off during the concert may have even been what prompted grandma to try to instill in me some appreciation for classical music. Eventually I learned Perlman and Williams worked together often and that Perlman was sometimes featured in Williams' movie scores. Over the years I came to really appreciate him, and particularly his performance of the theme to *Schindler's List*. It's a moving piece, and can bring one to tears—especially considering it is partnered with a story from the Jewish Holocaust.

If forced to pick a favorite piece composed by Williams, I'd probably pick the aforementioned theme from *Schindler's List*. I can hear the theme now. As the violin comes in my eyebrows furrow and raise. My head begins an involuntary sway back and forth ever so gently with each emotional note. I'm not sad, but I can feel the sadness in the tone. The piece invites me to cry.

As Mr. Williams arrived on stage on that May evening, the audience met him with an appropriate amount of raucous applause. With the same gesture all conductors have used throughout history, he picked up his baton, thereby directing the audience to fall silent. The caricature of orchestra conductors is of a person with hands flying around, shirts coming untucked, hair becoming disheveled from the rapid motion of arms flying everywhere. This couldn't be further from the actual experience most times. Williams was sitting. The baton seemed to be in a dual state where the conductor was holding it with such tenderness that you thought he might drop it, but it also seemed to be a permanent extension of his arm, which just rolled with the music ever so gently. As the score called for the music to get louder his arms would just roll bigger, never more violent. It was as if he was just there for a ride on the sound waves of the orchestral ocean. Only just before his boat was hit by a wave, he would point at it and tell it how high it was allowed to roll. And the sea of sound was so responsive, as if every member of the orchestra knew just what the master wanted and began producing the desired result just milliseconds before Williams asked for it and his conducting arms would just roll with the wave of music we all heard. The interplay was fascinating to me. The orchestra just *knew* what to do. And they did it so well.

Finally, after a few pieces, it was time to introduce the special guest performer for the evening and Williams turned to address the audience. Jazz singer Diane Reeves was scheduled to perform. I'm certain Diane would have been a treat, but on this night fate had more than a treat in store.

"I hope you don't mind that we have a change in our program tonight," Williams began. "A friend of mine is here and has been so gracious as to agree to share with us tonight."

138

The room kind of stirred a bit and I think most of the people in the audience were thinking the same thing I was thinking. *"Please let it be Perlman! Please let it be Perlman! Please let it be Perlman!"*

It was.

"Ladies and gentlemen, Itzhak Perlman!" he said gesturing stage right.

I cried. Seriously. I looked at my wife in disbelief, teared up, and cried. Not a heaving sobs kind of cry, but the little sniffle and wipe-the-tears-away-before-anyone-sees-them and have-a-little-cry-with-yourself kind of cry. Joy was looking at me like I was a bit crazy for caring so much. She'd have preferred a Dixie Chicks concert. But her face also beamed with happiness. As fantastic wives do, she had found a way to provide me with a lifetime memory.

Granted, these days we tend to over use superlatives. But Perlman's performance of *Schindler's List*, while being accompanied by The Boston Pops, who were being directed by John Williams—the guy who wrote the score—was everything I had hoped it would be. This alone is saying a lot, because I had allowed my emotions to set my expectations for the moment. You know how you might look up to a celebrity you've never met and place them on a pedestal like they can do no wrong? When you have the opportunity to meet the celebrity in real life, all those expectations are at risk, because you've set a difficult standard to meet. This is the scenario I'd created for a movie score. My expectations were that it would stir emotions within me, that it would be heartrending and inspirational. But when the performance arrived at our meeting place, it was on its best behavior and refused to disappoint. From the first four notes of the woodwinds, to the introductory harp, to the music flowing out of Perlman's Stradivarius violin. It was so good. I cried some more. Williams conducting. Perlman playing. The orchestra affirming the masters in their midst with harmonizing obedience. My wife holding my hand as the tones struck my own tympanic membranes. I'd dreamed of what the moment might have been, but for once my dreams had fallen short of reality.

The nature of dreams is that they can't live forever. Perlman finished and returned backstage. It was time for the *Phantom Menace* live world premiere. What I was initially so thrilled to be a part of was now simple cuddle time. Don't get me wrong, it was nice to be there for the first live performance of the most recent *Star Wars* score, but the apex moment of the evening had passed. As I reflect now, so much came together all at once, creating a moment of personal transcendence.

On that evening in May, sitting in Boston's Symphony Hall, I was immersed in the creative capacity of mankind. At some point in history for reasons known only to the guiding forces of the universe, somebody followed their inspirational inkling to create the screenplay for *Star Wars*.

Even the best screenplay performed by the most talented actors is lacking without a musical score. The score brings rhythm and emotion to the story, but is useless without master musicians to breathe life into it. Musicians whose years of dedication to their art yielded the knowledge of just how much life-giving breath to pass through the woodwinds and brass, or just how tenderly to pull the bow across the strings, and how hard to beat rhythm into the heartbeat of the percussion. They bring the notes to life through master-crafted instruments, which ultimately bring meaning to the notes on the page.

Just as musical talent worked to create the music, my family had worked to provide my appreciation of the same. Mom and Grandma insisting I attend classical concerts as I grew up, and not giving up on me when I protested or fell asleep, was no small victory. Grandma showed a certain amount of insight to pique my interest as a young lad. She constructed memories by dragging me to see classical music performances including maestro Itzhak Perlman. I'm sure my mother feels the thousands of dollars spent on twelve or so years of piano lessons were wasted. I was even kind of good at playing the piano, but I hated the work it took to bring about the goodness. However, an unintended consequence of my belief that practicing is a tedious task is my staunch appreciation for people who stick with it. I recognized then and I recognize now that thousands of hours went into providing that evening for that one night for me. O*ne night* when all the pieces were pulled together by my young, well-meaning wife. It all came together to create what some might call the perfect moment. But I'm not sure

I'd call it that. Perfection implies there is a limit to where goodness may go no further. Who am I to say that's what happened on that evening? I'll say this though—the universe conspired, and the participants responded to work and bring about something that was so good.

I can't help but consider if creating goodness is what life is all about. I remember the creation story I learned growing up in a Christian family. I suppose I can get caught up in a discussion of creation versus evolution, but I'm not sure that was the author's point. Seems to me there was more going on in the ancient literature. Several times in the story God moves in a creative capacity, then He (please pardon the patriarchal understanding of God—old habits die hard) declares it good. Light and day—good. Land which was separate from waters—good. Plants—good. Seasons, days, years, stars and other lights in the sky—good. Animals and fish—good. Even humans were considered good. All of the good worked together to create something better. In fact, as the story goes, the only time God didn't see something as good was when he determined man being alone was bad. So God created a second human—a woman. It strikes me that once this happened humanity could procreate. Or as I like to think of it, create like a pro.

I'm 43 years old and have only begun to appreciate my relationship with creation and making good stuff. I was always concerned with getting good grades so I could go to a good college which would provide a good education so I could get a good job with a good paycheck so I could live the good life. But none of that stuff *felt* good. It never felt like I was creating something. It felt like I was meeting expectations (except that I was usually failing at it). The goodness about creation might be in that when you create, it's ok to fail because nothing is at risk. When you don't create something pleasing to you, you just do it again. That time God didn't like what he created when he created man, he simply created again to make it good.

Now that I'm writing and have decided to create prose for people to read, I know I'm going to have to do it over, and over, and over, and over before I make something that is good. Then, when I'm happy with it, I'll show it to someone else who's probably better than me at writing and they will show me how it can still be better than it was when I felt it was good. So I press on—reworking creation to provide the best I can for, well, all of you. Perhaps someday I'll get good at it and provide a moment of warmth in the heart of my reader the way the John Williams did for me. The way Itzhak Perlman did for me. The way the percussionist, the many violinists, the many brass players, all the musicians did for me on that night of May in 1999.

The concert on that evening started at 7 p.m., but the experience began years before when the small child picked up a violin and drew the bow over the A-string to create a gawd-awful screech for the first time. It began when the percussionist picked up a drumstick and rapped on that single snare drum and banged out a headache for their parents for the first time. Or when the trumpet student produces her first loud, BLAAAAT. None of it was pretty, but it was creation, so it was good. Then, somewhere else, there was a writer who was fascinated by science fiction and wrote story after story, which ended up in the wastebasket. Those early drafts weren't compelling, but they were creation, so they were good. There was the budding composer who drew squiggly lines and dots on ledger paper over and over until he got the hang of it. For much of the 20th century, people who didn't know each other were working in untold places across the globe to produce their art, hone their craft, and simply create. That is how the best night of my life came to be. Through a dedication to creation, without any thought of...well, me.

CONTRIBUTORS

BOB BALESTRI has been an exclusive contributor to Getty Images/ iStockphoto since 2005, picking up from his earlier photography efforts while in Bladensburg High School before being diverted by a college degree and the need to earn a living. He and his spouse Marcia have travelled the entire globe photographing wildlife, landscapes, and urban scenes. His work can be viewed at: https://www.istockphoto. com/portfolio/joesboy.

SHIRLEY J. BREWER graduated from careers in bartending, palm-reading, and speech therapy. She serves as poet-in-residence at Carver Center for Arts & Technology in Baltimore, Maryland, and also teaches creative writing workshops to seniors. Recent poems garnish *Barrow Street*, *Comstock Review*, *Plainsongs*, *Poetry East*, *Slant*, and other journals. Shirley's poetry books include *A Little Breast Music*, Passager Books (2008); *After Words*, Apprentice House (2013); and *Bistro in Another Realm*, Main Street Rag (2017). www.apoeticlicense.com

JAMES BURD BREWSTER is author of the *Glad To Do It!* (www. GladToDoIt.net), *Pete and Petey*, and *Steve and Stevie* picture book series and president of J2B Publishing (J2BLLC.com), an Indie Press publishing enjoyable poetry and "Good Books for Young Boys and Girls." Jim's works have appeared in the *Pen-in-Hand* newsletter and the *Connections* literary magazine, and his books have been accepted at the Baltimore Book Festival, Gaithersburg Book Festival, and Kensington Day of the Book.

KATIE SPIVEY BREWSTER was raised in Wilmington, North Carolina, learned to body surf at Wrightsville Beach, married Jim Brewster, and raised and homeschooled five children (Ben, Luke, Rachel, Andrew, and Sam). She authored two picture books, *Aunt Louise Comes to Visit*, a story in rhyme, and *Feast of Memories*, as well as *Sparks Fly Upward*, a collection of original poems. She is Nana to seven grandchildren (Connor, Levi, Micah, Judah, Felicity, Seth, and Gideon).

CAROL CASEY lives in Betterton, Maryland, a small town located three miles north of Still Pond, where the Sassafras River meets the Chesapeake Bay. She returned to the Eastern Shore after working as a writer and editor in Washington, D.C., and living in Baltimore. When not gardening, enjoying the beach, or attempting to learn ancient Greek, she writes poetry, satirical academic fiction, and murder mysteries. She can be reached at canarycourt@gmail.com.

WALTER F. CURRAN is a retired Merchant Mariner. He has sailed and worked on the docks in Boston, Philadelphia, Baltimore, Jacksonville, and San Juan, Puerto Rico. A member of the Eastern Shore Writers Association, Maryland Writers Association, and Rehoboth Beach Writer's Guild, Walt has self-published two novels, *Young Mariner* and *On to Africa*, with the third of the trilogy, *Bombs Aweigh: On to Vietnam*, to be published in August 2019. He has also published a book of poetry, *Slices of Life: Cerebral Spasms of the Soul*. His website is www.walterfcurran.com.

KRISTIN DAVIS is a poet and former journalist based in Washington, D.C., and Maine. She leads workshops and retreats in contemplative meditation and enjoys choral singing and word games. Her journalism has appeared in *Kiplinger's Magazine*, *Reader's Digest*, *Redbook*, *U.S. News and World Report*, and the *Washington Post*, and her poetry in *What Rough Beast* and *Piebald Poems*.

BETH DULIN is a writer and artist living on the Eastern Shore of Maryland. A graduate of The New School's Eugene Lang College, she works as a freelance copy editor and an elementary reading and math tutor. She is the author and co-creator of *Truce*, a limited edition artists' book, in the collections of the Brooklyn Museum of Art and the Museum of Modern Art. To learn more, visit her online at www. bethdulin.com.

Winner of the 2018 *Gigantic Sequins* Poetry Contest, selected to attend the Delaware Division of the Arts 2016 Seashore Writers Retreat, and nominated for a Pushcart Prize, KARI ANN EBERT is working on her first poetry collection, *Alphabet of Mo(u)rning*. Her poetry has appeared in *Mojave River Review*, *Philadelphia Stories*, *The Broadkill Review*, *Gargoyle*, *Gravel*, and several anthologies. She lives in Dover, Delaware, and has two children who are also writers.

IRENE FICK's first and second books, *The Wild Side of the Window*, Main Street Rag 2018 and *The Stories We Tell*, The Broadkill Press 2014, each received first place awards from the National Federation of Press Women. Her poem, *Off Season*, this year received NFPW's first place honor. Irene's poems have been published in journals such as *Poet Lore*, *Gargoyle*, *The Broadkill Review*, and (forthcoming) *The Delmarva Review*. She lives in Lewes and is active in two writers' groups.

JUNE FORTE's short stories, personal essays, articles, and photographs have been featured in literary journals, magazines, newspapers, and anthologies. Her nonfiction writing and photographs have appeared in daily, weekly, and monthly newspapers and magazines. Past president of the Virginia Writers Club, she also served on the Poetry Society of Virginia's Advisory Board. She established the Poet Laureate position in Prince William County, Virginia, in 2014. June enjoys the writing challenge of style and format hopping.

ELISSA GORDON lives in Fruitland, Maryland, and works at the Center for International Education at the University of Maryland

Eastern Shore. She has appeared in print in *Lips*, *The Edison Literary Review*, *Bohemia Art & Literary Journal*, *River Poets Journal*, *Windmills* (Australia), online in *Kind of a Hurricane Press*, *Shot Glass Journal*, and *Short, Fast, and Deadly*, where she was also featured in two of their *Best of* print collections.

FRANK E HOPKINS writes realistic fiction, including four novels: *The Billion Dollar Embezzlement Murders*; *Abandoned Homes: Vietnam Revenge Murders*, which won first place in the mystery/thriller category in the Maryland Writers Association 2018 novel contest; *The Opportunity*; and *Unplanned Choices*. Frank's collection of short stories, *First Time*, won second place for a single-author collection in the Delaware Press Association's 2017 Communication contest. He belongs to ESWA, MWA, RBWG, and the Mystery Writers of America.

ANN HYMES has a B.A. in English from Mills College and an M.A. in English from Washington College. She has had numerous nonfiction essays published on *The Christian Science Monitor* Home Forum page. Her book, *Shadow of Whimsy: A Cape Cod Love Story*, was published by Secant Publishing. The novel is available in different formats, including audio. A sequel will be published by Secant in the Spring of 2020. Ann can be reached at whimsytowers@gmail.com.

MARILYN JANUS was raised on the New Jersey shore in Highlands and now lives on the Delaware shore in Dagsboro. As a church musician and writer since childhood, words and music have formed and informed her life. She considers her five grandchildren to be her best gig yet. Her short story "Firewalking" will appear in the 2019 edition of *Delmarva Review*. This is her first poetry in print.

CAROLINE KALFAS is a former newspaper journalist who lives in Woolwich Township, New Jersey. She helped establish the *Watering Can*, a seasonal newsletter for the Woolwich Community Garden. Her essay "Soggy Tomato Sandwiches" appeared in the *2018 Bay to Ocean* anthology. A graduate of North Carolina State University in Raleigh, she is a member of several writers' groups and organizations, including the Eastern Shore Writers Association. To read more of her essays go to carolinechatter.wordpress.com.

ADRIANNE LASKER has spent her professional career working in the corporate world doing marketing, P.R., and policy development. A lifelong lover of books and the creative process, she has been enthralled by the ability of her favorite authors to send readers on thrilling journeys. The dream of writing has now become a reality with this first-ever published piece.

Following graduation from the United States Merchant Marine Academy ('62) and seafaring in Asian waters, DEN LEVENTHAL studied China's language, history, and culture at the University of Pennsylvania and National Taiwan University. This led to a 30-year career as a China business development specialist. His experiences were memorialized in his book *How to Leap a Great Wall in China: The China Adventures of a Cross Cultural Trouble-Shooter* (2014). His other publications include *Sino-Judaic Studies: Whence and Whither* (1985), *The Chess of China* (1978), and articles in *Points East*, *Power Ships*, and *Words of Many Colors*.

BARBARA LOCKHART is the recipient of two Maryland State Arts Council Awards for excerpts from her novel, *Requiem for a Summer Cottage*, and her short stories. Winner of a silver medal from the Independent Publishers Book Award for her historical novel, *Elizabeth's Field*, and finalist in the National Indie Excellence Book Awards for her collection of short stories, *The Night is Young*, she is also the author of four children's books. Her website is barbaramarielockhart.com.

MELISSA MATTIE's life is an astonishing poster of grace and testament to God's power and love. She was, simply put, a very lost soul who is now found. Having gone through the furnace in her life and coming out unharmed by the fire, her biggest passion in life is to go and tell everyone of what God has done for her. She travels to different events to share her powerful message in her book, *Something Better*. Mattie resides in Berlin, Maryland, with her three children.

CLAIRE MCCABE teaches creative writing at the University of Delaware, where she is faculty advisor for the student literary annual, *Caesura*. McCabe earned bachelor's degrees in Journalism and Literature from Virginia Commonwealth University. She completed a master's degree in Linguistics at the University of Delaware, and an M.F.A. in Creative Writing: Poetry from the Solstice Program at Pine Manor College. She splits her time between homes in Newark, Delaware, and Fair Hill, Maryland.

NANCY MCCLOY lives with her husband in Still Pond, Maryland, and is a retired special educator. After retiring, she joined a local writer's group and was included in two self-published collections. Currently, she is a member of a small poetry group in Chestertown and has had three poems, one an honorable mention, included in two Art of Stewardship exhibits at River Arts in Chestertown. She was honored to be included in the 2018 *Bay to Ocean* Anthology.

SARAH MCGREGOR lives on the eastern seaboard with her husband, two daughters, and an assortment of dogs, cats, and horses. She's discovered the best stories come to her while running or sitting on a tractor. When all hell isn't breaking loose on the farm, she likes to travel. A lifelong equestrian, she's been told she's been around the proverbial barn enough times to portray it authentically. Follow her on Instagram at sbs.mcgregor and on her website, sarahsmcgregor.com.

S. B. MERROW lives in Baltimore, Maryland, where she writes poems and repairs concert flutes for professional musicians. Recently, her work has been accepted by *Salamander*, *Nimrod International Journal*, *Tishman Review*, *Gyroscope Review*, *Passager*, *Free State Review*, and other journals. She was a finalist in the *Naugatuck River Review*'s 2018 contest. Her chapbook *Unpacking the China* was the 2016 winner of the QuillsEdge Press chapbook competition.

A lifelong resident of the Eastern Shore of Maryland, L. L. POWELL enjoys crafting stories under the close supervision of her four black cats. She holds a B.A. in Creative Writing from Southern New Hampshire University. When she's not churning out pages, Powell can often be found performing with the Caroline Association of Theater. She is a proud member of the Maryland Writer's Association and the Eastern Shore Writer's Association. Her website is llpowellauthor.com; she's on Instagram at @llpowellauthor and on Facebook.

RUSSELL REECE's poems, stories and essays have appeared in a variety of journals and anthologies. Russ has received fellowships in literature from The Delaware Division of the Arts and the Virginia Center for the Creative Arts. He has received Best of the Net nominations, awards from the Delaware Press Association, the Faulkner-Wisdom competition and others. Russ lives in rural Sussex County near Bethel, Delaware, on the beautiful Broad Creek. You can learn more at his website, russellreece.com.

While writing professionally for five decades, WILLIE SCHATZ has covered business for *The Washington Post* and sports for *The New York Daily News* and *The Morning Call* (Allentown, Pennsylvania). Willie is an editor, an executive writing coach for clients seeking to strengthen their writing skills, and the Artist-in-Residence of the Writers' Group at *Street Sense*, a biweekly Washington, D.C., street newspaper. He and spouse Molly divide their time between the District and Lewes, Delaware. Find his work at www.schatzgroup.com.

JEFFREY SCOTT, M. Ed, is a husband and father of two. His career has afforded him the opportunity to spend time in higher education, contract security, police communications, and welding. The New England native relocated to Salisbury, Maryland, in 2016, and is glad to have discovered more time to write on the lower, slower, Eastern Shore. Primarily by means of memoir writing, he enjoys discussing his faith (re)construction, and lessons learned along life's way.

Selections of CATHERINE R. SEELEY's poetry have appeared among the works of prominent New York women artists for a gallery exhibit entitled "Women of Spirit." With a background in health care administration, medical ethics, and in crisis, grief and transition, Catherine's professional writings have been about bereavement, palliative care, and health care ethics. After writing her first novel, *Mea Culpa*, Catherine now lives and writes in Easton, Maryland.

TERRI SIMON's poetry chapbook *Ghosts of My Own Choosing* was published by Flutter Press in 2017. Her work has appeared in *The Avenue*, *Third Wednesday*, *Poetry Quarterly*, *Rat's Ass Review*, *Mused*, and other print and online journals, as well as several anthologies. She received honorable mention in the Kind of a Hurricane Press Editor's Choice for 2015. She lives in Laurel, Maryland, and can be found at http://www.terricsimon.com or on Twitter as @terricsimon.

PEGGY WARFIELD was born and raised in the Baltimore area. She graduated from McDaniel College with a B.A. in English and taught high school English in Baltimore County and Baltimore City. She moved to Ocean City, Maryland, with her late husband, Bob Warfield, in 1972. Two children and three grandchildren complete her family circle. Peggy's memoir piece, "Maryland, My Maryland," was published in the 2019 Maryland Writers' Association anthology, *30 Ways to Love Maryland*.

2019 EDITORIAL BOARD

ELLEN KRAWCZAK is a transplanted New Yorker who lives on Maryland's Eastern Shore. In her work life she was a paralegal, substitute teacher, real estate settlement officer, and trainer. She is now retired and spends her days reading and watching the ducks glide up and down the St. Martin River.

SUSAN PARKER is a retired journalist. She worked 28 years at *The Daily Times*, *Delmarva Now*, and Gannett Newspapers, serving as an editor, reporter, and community liaison. She lives in Salisbury, Maryland. In her spare time she plays violin occasionally at Poplar Hill Mansion and St. Francis de Sales Church, crochets, and enjoys gardening, family gatherings, and her cats.

Co-Managing Editor EMILY RICH has edited nonfiction for literary reviews for over five years. She writes mainly memoir and essay. Her work has been published in a number of small presses including *Little Patuxent Review*, *r.kv.ry*, *The Pinch*, and *Hippocampus*. Her essays have been listed as notables in *Best American Essays* 2014 and 2015. She teaches memoir writing at the Writers Center in Bethesda and the Lighthouse Literary Guild at Salisbury University.

DONNA ROTHERT is a retired corporate executive and former high school teacher, who has had a lifelong love of words: puzzles, fiction, non-fiction, poetry, drama. She travels weekly between the Eastern Shore and Washington, D.C., and is currently working on her memoir while making intermittent forays into essays, short stories, and flash fiction. Her essays appeared in the 30th anniversary anthology of the Maryland Writers' Association, *30 Ways to Love Maryland*, and a short story is to be included in the Rehoboth Beach upcoming *Beach Dreams* story collection.

Co-Managing Editor PAT VALDATA is a poet and fiction writer. Her poetry book about women aviation pioneers, *Where No Man Can*

Touch, won the 2015 Donald Justice Prize. Pat teaches creative writing for the University of Maryland Global Campus (formerly UMUC) and the Lighthouse Literary Guild at Salisbury University. She and her husband Bob Schreiber live in Crisfield, Maryland. Learn more at www.patvaldata.com.

Guest Editor GREGG WILHELM directs the MFA and BFA in Creative Writing Programs at George Mason University in Fairfax, Virginia.

Made in the USA
Lexington, KY
10 December 2019

58328137R00095